WHAT STUDENTS WANT FROM THEIR PSHE IN SECONDARY SCHOOL

This thought-provoking text stems from the voices of young people in secondary schools, and what they want from their PSHE education. The book focuses on personal development, an aspect of PSHE that is often side-lined in favour of a more topic-based approach, to consider how PSHE lessons can help young people build the knowledge, skills and character necessary to navigate a fast-changing world.

Informed by feedback collected from over 10,000 students on their experiences of PSHE and personal development education, chapters provide suggestions for moving towards solutions that will help teachers improve provision in what is often a tricky topic to teach. The book discusses how the fast-paced changes in today's world make PSHE particularly difficult to teach and offers advice and guidance on what best practice looks like in such an ever-moving field, along with signposts to further reading and supporting lesson plans.

With activities in each chapter to build knowledge and develop skills which students will find useful throughout school and into future study and employment, this book is essential reading for any teacher looking for further guidance in the secondary PSHE classroom.

Angela Milliken-Tull has over 25 years' experience working in education and public health. She has worked in the secondary and university sector and is a public health specialist. She has held regional and national roles developing a range of training programmes and resources and is committed to health improvement through effective education delivered by confident, empowered teachers. Angela is the Director and Co-Founder of Chameleon PDE.

Access your Online Resources

What Students Want from their PSHE in Secondary School is accompanied by a number of printable online materials, designed to ensure this resource best supports your professional needs.

To download printable copies of the end-of-chapter resources, go to https://resourcecentre.routledge.com/speechmark, click on the cover of this book and answer the question prompt using your copy of the book to gain access to the online content.

To download the accompanying lesson packs and CPD sessions, go to https://www.chameleonpde.com/book_resources

WHAT STUDENTS WANT FROM THEIR PSHE IN SECONDARY SCHOOL

How Listening to Student Voice Can Help you Build a Great Programme

Angela Milliken-Tull

LONDON AND NEW YORK

Designed cover image: Getty Images

First published 2025
by Routledge
4 Park Square, Milton Park, Abingdon, Oxon OX14 4RN

and by Routledge
605 Third Avenue, New York, NY 10158

Routledge is an imprint of the Taylor & Francis Group, an informa business

© 2025 Angela Milliken-Tull

Some figures in this book have been created by the author using Canva

The right of Angela Milliken-Tull to be identified as author of this work has been asserted in accordance with sections 77 and 78 of the Copyright, Designs and Patents Act 1988.

All rights reserved. The purchase of this copyright material confers the right on the purchasing institution to photocopy or download pages which bear the support material icon and a copyright line at the bottom of the page. No other parts of this book may be reprinted or reproduced or utilised in any form or by any electronic, mechanical, or other means, now known or hereafter invented, including photocopying and recording, or in any information storage or retrieval system, without permission in writing from the publishers.

Trademark notice: Product or corporate names may be trademarks or registered trademarks, and are used only for identification and explanation without intent to infringe.

British Library Cataloguing-in-Publication Data
A catalogue record for this book is available from the British Library

ISBN: 978-1-032-72461-4 (hbk)
ISBN: 978-1-032-72460-7 (pbk)
ISBN: 978-1-032-72463-8 (ebk)

DOI: 10.4324/9781032724638

Typeset in Interstate
by Apex CoVantage, LLC

Access the Support Material: https://resourcecentre.routledge.com/speechmark

CONTENTS

Acknowledgements	vi
Foreword	vii
Introduction	ix
1 **PSHE challenges and health ambitions**	1
2 **Don't keep telling us what we already know: Monitoring progress in PSHE**	10
3 **Not another video, worksheet, quiz . . .: Injecting variety into PSHE lessons**	27
4 **We are uniquely transient: A brief introduction to the amazing teenage brain**	48
5 **If you don't take this seriously, why should I?: The importance of role models**	65
6 **So, what has this got to do with me?: The importance of relevance in PSHE**	81
7 **Spare me the lecture!: Effective pedagogy in PSHE**	103
8 **This is so embarrassing!: Managing student and staff embarrassment in PSHE**	119
9 **We want more life skills!**	138
10 **Teacher wellbeing?: How can you stop your bucket from overflowing?**	153
Bibliography	164
Index	166

ACKNOWLEDGEMENTS

The voices of teachers referenced in this book and the much wider group I am privileged to work with regularly have been fundamental to developing the thinking and content that has gone into every chapter of this book. I am always grateful for suggestions and challenges to move the world of PSHE a little bit further in its journey.

The experts' voices referenced offer value and insight to areas of specialism within PSHE, and the other authors whose work appears in the Further Reading sections show passion and insight that inspires, and I am truly thankful.

Students' voices are at the heart of this book, and I thank them for their honesty. With them, I could delve into their needs from PSHE and offer suggestions and potential solutions to the reader.

I thank the publishing team at Routledge for supporting and guiding me through this new endeavour. I am grateful for the opportunity to share my thoughts on this critical but often overlooked curriculum area with teachers across the UK and beyond.

Finally, I would like to thank my family and friends who have listened, supported and always given me perspective on what's important and helped me be the best version of myself.

FOREWORD

I am delighted and not a little flattered to be able to provide a short introduction to this excellent book.

Since the notion of PSHE education was first introduced in the 1990s, we have moved, sometimes effectively, sometimes rather shambolically, to improve provision. We know from increasing research evidence that, when taught well, PSHE education can improve the physical health and emotional wellbeing of children and young people and contributes to their academic attainment.

I was in Westminster Hall when the then schools minister, Jim Knight, announced that PSHE would be statutory, and I wept. Those years of campaigning, cajoling and providing evidence felt vindicated. Unfortunately, that was in 2008, and a change of government meant that it was more than a decade before this finally came to pass.

In 2013 Ofsted reported that in 40% of schools, PSHE education was 'not yet good enough'. More recently, findings from the Department of Education on implementing the 2020 R(S)HE curriculum guidance in schools paint a different picture. Teachers and school leaders are responding to the statutory expectations and moral imperative to provide the necessary life skills to children and young people, many of whom are going to live into the twenty-second century.

This gradual evolution is, in no small part, thanks to some of the authors here, dozens of others and the thousands of teachers across the country who are working so hard to implement these changes and meet the challenges we all face.

All of our pupils, irrespective of their educational setting, from early years right through until they leave full-time education, have an entitlement to high-quality learning and teaching in PSHE education. Knowledge is important but of equal value are the attitudes and attributes and the skills that are necessary to flourish in a fast-changing world. They need to be able to identify and name their emotions and to be able to manage their relationships with increasing confidence and competence. Some of these relationships may become intimate and lifelong and need to be safe and fulfilling.

Other relationship skills are also needed in the workplace and society. Children and young people also need to develop the skills of resilience, compassion, empathy and oracy to manage the personal and global challenges that we already know about and those that we do not even yet realise are problems.

This book, and the ethos behind it, contributes another step towards achieving this crucial moral, social and educational purpose.

John Rees
PSHE Advisor
October 2024

INTRODUCTION

I have worked with teachers and students throughout my career, as a teacher and a trainer and within a public health team. The links between education and health are well established. Yet PSHE, the curriculum area with an excellent opportunity to influence health choices and positively impact academic achievement needs, is often sidelined and given less time than it needs or students deserve. Even when schools work hard to establish a good quality PSHE programme, there is frequently little regard for genuinely listening to student voices, and teachers need to be more prepared to deliver a subject area that they have had little training in and often changes very quickly.

Students' voices are at the heart of this book, and by listening to what they tell us they do and don't want in PSHE classes, we can be better prepared to provide relevant, exciting and adaptive lessons that will equip them with the knowledge and skills to prepare them for the future.

This book will help you better understand what students want and provide ideas and solutions that, combined with your teaching skills, will make PSHE more enjoyable for you and your students.

How to get the most from this book

What Students Want from their PSHE in Secondary School aims to provide you with a concise overview of what a practical and relevant PSHE programme should look like from a student's perspective. Whether you are new to teaching PSHE or have recently taken on a PSHE leadership role, there will be ideas, suggestions and recommendations to support you in your role.

The evidence that underpins and informs much of the content is data collected from thousands of secondary school-age students from a range of educational settings. Each chapter from 2 to 9 uses often-repeated student comments to frame the chapter's content and serves as a stimulus to delve a little deeper into what has led to the comment. This leads on to practical tips and solutions that can be quickly put into practice.

Each chapter follows the same structure, allowing you to become familiar with the layout quickly.

Discussion

Discussion stems from data collected from students and comments they have made about PSHE pulling key themes together to help better understand concerns raised and unpick what this means for your PSHE practice.

Data, evidence and research

The main source of evidence being used to inform this book is the student voice data collected by Chameleon PDE. Each year responses are collected from many thousands of students from schools in the UK and a few international schools. Results are collated each year and trends monitored year on year. Schools completing the survey can compare their own data against the amalgamated dataset. There are examples throughout the chapters referring to this data.

Other sources of evidence are included as well as some popular models used in education and psychology. However, this book primarily focuses on how student voice can help you gain practical insight into how to deliver needs-based PSHE rather than taking a theoretical approach.

Children, young people and research

When looking for evidence-based research about PSHE generally and some of the topics within the PSHE curriculum there's not a great deal to draw on. You may come across a few research papers on specific interventions but even these are relatively limited compared with the wealth of research available for other aspects of education.

There are some obvious and understandable reasons for this.

1. It can be difficult to obtain ethics approval to undertake research with young people.

2. The fast pace of change across many themes within PSHE means that research findings date very quickly. Sometimes the findings are out of date before they are published.

3. Longitudinal research often stretches across many years or even decades. When studying adolescents this is a challenge as they are only at this development stage for a relatively short period.

4. The gold standard of research is randomized control trials. These are expensive and take time, and obtaining ethical approval for use with children is challenging, especially if there are any invasive procedures involved such as collecting personal data or taking blood or other samples.

5. Cause and effect can be difficult to 'prove' when working with any group but can be particularly challenging when working with children and young people. This is due to the many influences they are exposed to that can change quickly, making it difficult to ascertain what has had the greatest impact on whatever is being measured, e.g. a behaviour change.

When building evidence about what works (or doesn't) in your PSHE programme, regular data collection and modification of your programme is likely to be the most effective approach. This means that your PSHE lead with support from others is engaging in an ongoing process of action research.

Suggestions and tips

In addition to discussing the theme of the chapter there are suggestions and tips you can put into your everyday practice that address the issues raised by students. There are further opportunities to implement these suggestions by using the supporting resources that accompany each of the main chapters.

> **CASE STUDY**
>
> Where appropriate, chapters are supported by a case study written by a teacher or other expert sharing their views and experiences on the topic covered in the chapter. They share insights, ideas and observations from lived experience, knowledge and practice. This helps contextualise and bring to life the issues discussed in the chapter.

KEY TAKEAWAYS

Each chapter concludes with three key takeaways. These ask you to

Acknowledge
Accept
Aspire

The first two aim to help ground the discussion and provide perspective. They will encourage you to acknowledge challenges and accept things that are out of your control. *Aspire* suggests areas of ambition for your PSHE programme based on the issues discussed in the chapter.

PERSONAL REFLECTION

It is useful to take some time to reflect and each chapter concludes with three questions for you to reflect on. The questions ask you to consider your setting and current practice. Some will challenge your thinking on PSHE. The aim is to help you consider how PSHE can potentially be enhanced to better meet the needs of students, support their development and help them build the skills that will benefit them in the future and develop character.

FURTHER READING

If you feel motivated to find out more on the topics covered in a chapter there are some suggestions for further reading. This includes books that have a more in-depth focus on a specific area as well as reports, articles and useful websites.

LESSON PACK

To help you better understand the themes and suggestions in each chapter there are signposts to a lesson pack or CPD resource for you to download and use in school. These can be accessed via the instructions at the front of this book.

RESOURCES

End of chapter additional resources provide activity suggestions, tools and extension idea to use in the classroom. These can also be downloaded by following the instructions at the front of this book.

1 PSHE challenges and health ambitions

Education is about more than young people learning the facts that will enable them to pass exams. The wider curriculum is a key element of young people's education experience. It should work alongside more traditional subjects to prepare students for the next stages of life, whether that's further educational endeavours or moving on to work or training.

The personal development curriculum offered by schools has been a significant component of inspection frameworks for many years. Since the 2019/20 academic year, it has been a statutory requirement for secondary state schools in England to deliver Relationships, Sex and Health Education (RSHE) as part of the wider Personal, Social, Health and Economic (PSHE) curriculum. In the often-quoted words of Sir Michael Marmot, author of multiple research papers and books on the social determinants of health state,

> It is not just that people with no education have worse health. People with a bit of education are somewhat better, with a lot of education it's even better. And with even more education it's better still. (Marmot, 2010)

Acknowledgement and inspection of this area were welcomed by most, not least of all, as there had been a long-standing campaign to include these topics as part of the statutory curriculum. However, this has also created a set of challenges.

Five key challenges will be discussed throughout this book alongside the issues raised by students about what they want from their PSHE lessons.

1. *Lack of expertise.* Most teachers are not 'experts' in topics outside of their main subject areas. Teacher training programmes provide little or no PSHE, yet many teachers are expected to deliver PSHE lessons.
2. *'Squeezed' curriculum.* The wider personal development curriculum is extensive. Students also cover many 'traditional' subjects, meaning that timetables become

increasingly squeezed, with little spare capacity to fit in more topics, even when there is a statutory obligation to do so.

3. *Fast pace of change.* Ever faster change is a key feature of modern life, and this creates a third challenge for delivering personal development and PSHE sessions to students. To be useful, lessons need to be relevant, up-to-date and engaging. While teachers are adept at creating engaging lessons, keeping PSHE knowledge up to date and relevant for different cohorts of students is not easy.

4. *Controversy.* Controversy is never far from some of the topics included in statutory RSHE, and therein lies a further challenge. While some teachers may be confident in their delivery of many topics within the PSHE curriculum, some areas send many running for the hills! It's not always possible to allow teachers to 'opt' out of the topics they feel uncomfortable with. An added concern is how parents might react to content that they may feel is inappropriate or where strongly held views are at odds with statutory expectations.

5. *Reputation of PSHE.* The final challenge is 'reputation'. No one wants to be associated with a subject that is regarded as superficial or a 'waste of time'. When senior leaders do not place all of the components of the wider personal development curriculum on an equal footing with other subjects, there is a danger that it will not be taken seriously by teachers, and this, of course, will filter down to students. So, parity is vital, and this must start at the top.

How this book will help you

Discussion, examples, case studies and some practical strategies will help teachers feel better prepared and confident about delivering engaging, relevant and up-to-date PSHE.

Many of the suggestions have been drawn from student input, and who better to inform this than the recipients of the education themselves?

Each chapter will delve into what students don't want in their PSHE lessons. We will aim to unpick what lies behind some of these comments and criticisms and suggest examples to help engage students with relevant and challenging PSHE that encourages curiosity, self-reflection, builds knowledge and enhances skills, values and attitudes. This will help you feel more confident about what makes PSHE sessions student-focused and supports the personal development that builds character and prepares young people for the next stage of education, training and the world of work.

Each chapter will conclude with a comprehensive lesson pack or teacher continuous professional development (CPD) to demonstrate and enhance the discussion in the chapter and give you resources to work with.

Long-term health outcomes and education

When talking about PSHE, the 'H' stands for health. There are very strong links between health and education, and the quote at the start of this chapter underscores this connection. Simply put, robust data at a population level demonstrate that better education leads to better long-term health. Of course, the factors associated with better educational outcomes are multifaceted, and barriers to accessing or making the most of educational opportunities are wide-ranging. Children from more deprived backgrounds do less well and in recent years social mobility has declined. This, of course, has an impact on long-term health outcomes.

Schools have a powerful role to play in health promotion, both in terms of general encouragement of aspiration for educational success, which by default will enable more young people to go on to lead healthier lives, and in terms of supporting healthy choices, which in turn will help children better access education.

To some extent, better education leading to better health can be turned on its head with the acknowledgement that better health will enable children to access better education. This will include having the knowledge and skills to make healthy choices, form supportive relationships, and manage emotions. Let's face it, if children are tired, hungry, unable to manage worries about other aspects of their lives, or experiencing mental ill-health, their ability to access education will be reduced.

Some barriers to accessing education are beyond the control of teachers, and specialist intervention is required. However, universal support that can help prevent the escalation of issues and, where possible, assist students in managing themselves as much as possible is a good ambition. An effective PSHE programme is part of this strategy. An excellent way to inform such a strategy is to listen to what students have to say.

The power of student voice

For many years, I have worked with teachers, public health experts and students to develop an effective student voice survey and analyse the resulting data and what it means for developing effective and impactful PSHE lessons. This has resulted in many thousands of student voices being captured, with amazingly consistent results emerging across the UK and beyond. As anyone familiar with teenagers will know, they often feel misunderstood and not listened to. Feedback can be scathing as they go through adolescence's physical and emotional changes.

One way to support students as they navigate this bumpy journey is to listen to them. This can be done through discussion and student council-type activities, but these methods alone will not capture the views of more introverted or non-communicative pupils, whose opinions and needs are, of course, as valid as those of their more confident or outspoken peers. An easy and effective way to achieve this is through an anonymous questionnaire.

Having listened to students, you have an obligation to respond to what has been shared. This not only affirms the value of the exercise but also provides an opportunity for meaningful engagement and a shared understanding of the areas where students may require more input. Conversely, it highlights the areas where they are already knowledgeable and competent and may only need a light touch. You can be confident that your lessons will be more relevant as you respond to what they have told you.

This bottom-up approach, as opposed to top-down, is recommended in many walks of life. As adults, it is more empowering to be involved in the decisions that affect us, and it is likely to lead to greater engagement and interest.

The second and often overlooked benefit of conducting a student survey is the opportunity to congratulate your students on the excellent decisions that most of them make!

Young people are often tarred with a very unflattering brush that is both unfair and, in most cases, untrue. Reinforcing the positive data around behaviour choice not only celebrates the choices of the majority, but it can also be protective. Social norms theory tells us that we naturally want to behave the same way as our peers. When considering teenagers, peer influence can be even stronger than in the general population.

As we delve into how to make PSHE lessons relevant, meaningful and enjoyable for students, it will be in conjunction with what has been learned from listening to many thousands of students and considering their choices, perceptions, and views.

This knowledge will help empower you to be the expert!

In many areas across the UK, there is expert advice available from Public Health teams and others to support schools with health-related activities and interventions, including PSHE. In the case study below a forward-thinking public health specialist shares her vision and aims for the 'healthy schools' she supports.

CASE STUDY

Caroline McAleese, Public Health Specialist: School-aged Children and Young People, Swindon Borough Council

Healthy schools create environments for pupils to learn, grow and thrive physically, emotionally and academically.

Evidence indicates that:

1. Pupils with better health and wellbeing are likely to achieve better academically.
2. Effective social and emotional competencies are associated with greater health and wellbeing, and better achievement.
3. The culture, ethos, and environment of a school influence the health and wellbeing of pupils and their readiness to learn.
4. A positive association exists between academic attainment and physical activity levels of pupils (Public Health, England, 2014).

To reduce inequalities and improve the life chances for young people, Swindon Healthy Schools supports schools to deliver a whole school approach to the health and wellbeing of their pupils, staff and parents and carers. We do this through:

- *Supporting schools to network* and offer peer support through a PSHE Leads Network, a Senior Mental Health Leads Network and an Affordable Schools Network. These networks are an opportunity for school staff to share good practice, offer tips and share resources. For example, schools have shared translated materials for families with English as an additional language and have shared tips on supporting pupils around emotionally based school non-attendance.

- *Supporting schools to gain Healthy Schools status* to improve pupil and staff wellbeing through the following awards:
    - Swindon Healthy Schools – bronze, silver and gold;
    - Swindon Schools Mental Health and Emotional Wellbeing;
    - Bath & North East Somerset, Swindon and Wiltshire Asthma Friendly Schools.

When they achieve one of the above awards, schools receive a logo or certificate and are highlighted in the Swindon Healthy Schools newsletter. We also inform schools of national awards available to them, such as Food for Life. Achieving these awards not only offers schools a framework to improve their practice, but it also strengthens their pupil voice and puts schools in good stead for Ofsted inspections.

- Encouraging and linking schools with *PSHE resources*, for instance, Chameleon PDE's resources library for secondary schools, which includes lesson and assembly plans, pupil voice surveys, videos and a parents' portal. Swindon Borough Council has funded schools to access these resources to contribute to COVID recovery until July 2024. Following positive feedback, we have since negotiated a discount for secondary schools and expect most secondary schools to continue subscribing to Chameleon PDE's resources library.

  Commissioning *vaping, smoking and cannabis workshops, resources and staff CPD* through Chameleon PDE. Secondary schools have been given resources to continue delivering these lessons in the classroom. The CPD in particular has ensured that this intervention is sustainable. Swindon Public Health Team is launching primary school resources, aimed at year 6, to complement this offer.

- Commissioning the *How are You? pupil voice survey*, which has offered invaluable guidance to public health strategy and shed light on social norms data that are used by PSHE teachers in the classroom. For example, recent data indicates that aspirations may be lower for Swindon pupils than nationally. This data will be discussed at a forthcoming headteachers' conference, which will have a theme of supporting aspirations. The findings have also indicated differences between genders and ethnic groups, such as confidence around reporting incidents relating to personal safety, types of bullying experienced, mental wellbeing and resilience, self-harm, receiving or sending inappropriate images, gambling, alcohol and vaping. The results will be discussed with schools and addressed through a current workstream to tackle a local need to better support boys regarding their mental health. Previous results have been integrated into several workstreams, including targeted work to improve RSHE in schools, which was highlighted by young people as lacking.

- *Providing a regular newsletter* to inform schools of resources, training and research findings to support the provision of healthy school settings.

- *Training school staff where there are identified needs*. For instance, in 2024, we worked with the Bladder and Bowel Nurse at Swindon Community Health Service to provide almost all primary, secondary and special schools with free online training on supporting pupils around their bladder and bowel health. We are also currently working through the recent How are You? survey findings to plan and signpost to relevant training for PSHE teachers.

- *Developing resources for parents and carers.* Schools are in an ideal position to support parents and carers with regard to their wellbeing, which also positively impacts their children. We recently provided a template document for schools to offer parents wishing to remove their children from aspects of relationships and sex education, along with a guide for parents and carers on discussing relationships and sex with their teenagers. We have supported primary schools in Swindon in accessing a free trial of Jigsaw Families, which provides an informal and safe environment to explore the challenges of being a parent. The programme aims to offer strategies to help meet families' needs through sessions delivered to 10 adults with their children, led by facilitators from the school who have been trained by Jigsaw.
- *Trialling a young mental health champions programme with five secondary schools*, two of which are special schools. An athlete mentor will train five young people in each of the five schools to develop a project to support their peers at school.

As readers of this book will be well aware, local authority budgets are limited, and so we work in partnership and creatively to provide the best offer we can to support Swindon schools in being healthy, given these constraints. We are currently reviewing our offer to consider how it can remain sustainable, particularly in light of these challenges.

On a personal note, I am particularly drawn to this work because childhood and adolescence are critical periods for physical, mental and emotional development. In particular, school-aged children are going through their formative years and spend so much time at school.

My background is in the voluntary sector, including community development, working with unpaid family carers and in women's services. I have witnessed and supported people regarding health inequalities and am passionate about creating an equitable playing field as early as possible; working in partnership around early intervention is a great step to ensure that, regardless of socioeconomic background, all children have the opportunity to thrive.

Schools, in particular, are well placed to provide a healthy setting for children and young people. As someone in their late 40s, I would say that my peers and I could probably share some stories of rather unhealthy aspects of our previous school settings from the 1980s and 1990s, and it's wonderful to see the shift over the years and to support the continuation of this movement. One of the biggest outcomes that I see in this work is the opportunities we can create for schools to network and support each other and share good practice around interventions that have worked well in their settings.

KEY TAKEAWAYS

Acknowledge that PSHE has an important role to play in supporting long-term health outcomes.

Accept the importance of capturing student voice to develop a 'bottom up' PSHE programme

Aspire to be a health-promoting school that strives to improve health outcomes for all young people by reducing the barriers to accessing the great education that will impact on life-long health,

---

PERSONAL REFLECTIONS

1. Is your school health-promoting?

2. What are the main barriers to some children accessing education in your school?

3. Is there anything you could do or aspire to do in your PSHE practice that would help improve access to education?

FURTHER READING

Public Health England (2024) The link between pupil health and wellbeing and attainment, https://assets.publishing.service.gov.uk/media/5a7ede2ded915d74e33f2eba/HT_briefing_layoutvFINALvii.pdf

If you are interested in finding out more about public health, health inequality and how this affects life chances, the two books below are a good start.

Marmot, Michael (2016) *The Health Gap*, Bloomsbury

Marmot, Michael (2007) *Status Syndrome*, Times Books

2 Don't keep telling us what we already know

Monitoring progress in PSHE

A common complaint from students is that some topics in PSHE are repeated multiple times. If this occurs in the same manner, understandably, it can become very dull; students switch off and assume that they already know everything about the topic being delivered.

However, recognising the title of a lesson topic that may have been covered to some extent previously and 'knowing' about it can be two very different things. If we compare this to a different curriculum area, for example, history, students might think they know about the First World War, but digging a little deeper will soon reveal how much knowledge they have retained. Can they connect their knowledge to contemporary issues, other curriculum areas or historical events? PSHE is no different. Add skills and values to the mix that are likely to sit alongside a given topic, and a student's assumption that they have already learned all there is to know about a topic will often fall by the wayside.

As educators, you play a pivotal role in addressing this issue. Your understanding and proactive approach can significantly impact student engagement.

Step 1 – Know which topics they think are repetitive

Collecting student data about PSHE can be very insightful. When datasets are sufficiently large they can demonstrate that some topics within the PSHE curriculum tend to receive far more attention than others (Chameleon PDE, 2024). This may be because the subjects are considered to be more critical, and often, the topics that students rank as being covered well are also viewed as somewhat repetitive.

Figure 2.1 provides some insight into the topics within the PSHE curriculum that students report as being 'good' or 'okay', when asked: 'How would you rate the PSHE/health and wellbeing lessons you have received in secondary school?' The options students can select are: 'good', 'ok', 'could be better' and 'poor/non-existent'

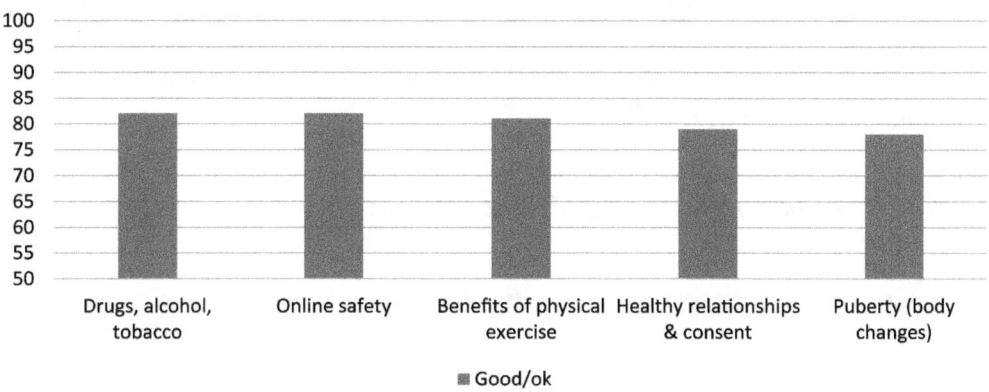

Figure 2.1 Top five PSHE topics

Drug, tobacco and alcohol education is in joint first place with online safety lessons. Students also report favourably on lessons promoting the benefits of physical activity. The physical changes that young people experience during puberty are further areas in which students report positively, and the final entry to the top five is lessons on healthy relationships and consent.

These data provide student-reported views on the topics expected to be delivered in a PSHE curriculum, with the main focus being on the statutory (RSHE) content. They are providing insight to the content delivered and implying their knowledge of these areas. Follow-up questions ask for written comments on areas they would like further input on.

There are a few things to consider when looking at the data.

1. Students are aged 11–14, and this group is generally more complimentary about PSHE than their older peers.
2. Some of the topics in the 'top 5' would have been delivered in primary school. For example, substances and puberty lessons are often given some focus towards the end of primary school.
3. Views about online safety are interesting. Students feel well-versed and competent in this area, yet we regularly hear about problems arising online. Does this suggest that students know about the dangers and precautions they can take but still make poor choices?
4. When we split puberty by physical and emotional changes, the latter is reported far less positively.

5. It's clear that schools are working hard to include health relationships and consent in PSHE, and consent is one area reported as being repetitive. However, the whole area of healthy relationships often concerns teachers and includes examples of disrespectful behaviour, misogyny, verbal bullying and homophobic and transphobic language.

Step 2 - Managing variability of student maturity when planning content

Conversely, some topics where students report good knowledge are criticised for being repetitive.

> we learned about puberty at primary school; we don't need it repeated every year in secondary school and have all gone through puberty!

Of course, physical and emotional maturity is very individual, but we can accept that it may become boring for the early developers.

We should also acknowledge that most, but not all, primary schools deliver puberty sessions. It is a topic that some teachers avoid, or they arrange a session with a school nurse, often slotted in towards the end of the summer term.

There is a great deal of variation in how students develop physically and emotionally throughout adolescence. This means that topics must be revisited to ensure that all students receive the necessary information at the right time. The trick is to repeat knowledge within different issues and contexts to present it from a fresh perspective. Students report that information on physical changes at puberty can become repetitive. However, many also report that there needs to be more time given to the emotional changes associated with puberty. A strategy to revisit puberty in a different guise could be to focus on emotional changes and task students with making the connections to the physical changes that they already know about. This provides an opportunity to take a different approach while still checking for gaps in knowledge about bodily changes.

Students claim that lessons about consent are repeated too frequently, and this is another area that can be revisited in a different context. There is an automatic assumption that consent refers to sexual consent, but, of course, there is a far wider meaning. With younger students, consent should encompass more everyday considerations. This will provide the foundations on which to build more adult content, including sexual consent. Older students can benefit from a more nuanced approach and delve into what active consent entails concerning intimate relationships.

Step 3 - Use qualitative data too!

Discussions with students or free text space on surveys are constructive ways to gain further insights into how your student body feels about PSHE lessons. As mentioned above, information on consent is often reported as repetitive. Yet, some (older) students share that they have experienced sexual activity where consent was not given. We have a disconnect between *knowing* what consent is and having the skills to actively request consent and fully understand when it has been granted or denied. Perhaps video resources are being used without opportunities for meaningful follow-up discussions, leading to missed learning opportunities.

LGBTQ+ education tends to polarise student views, with some reporting too much coverage and others not enough. You will know how much content is in your programme, and seeking student views about this often sensitive and controversial area will help you get the balance right for your students.

How to address this issue

Adding more LGBTQ+ content is straightforward as long as there is space in your programme to do so. If students report too much coverage you can also rebalance things, but what can you do if there are polarised views? Here are some suggestions for you to consider:

1. Weave a range of protected characteristics throughout lessons rather than have focused sessions on LGBTQ+, disability, etc. This is also a good way to address intersectionality, allowing consideration of multiple protected characteristics, e.g. being female and disabled and coming from an ethic minority group.
2. Case studies or scenarios to discuss relationships, for example, could use non-gendered names. In that way you are focusing on the topic rather than being side-tracked by sexuality.
3. Use progress and assessment as an opportunity to challenge students to consider protected characteristics, values, connections to previously covered work or the wider curriculum and how these relate to the topic being assessed. This is also a good way to encourage deeper learning.

Taking comments or feedback anonymously and providing a simple comments box where all students can post a comments sheet (which might be blank), often works more successfully than trying to collect feedback online. Equally difficult can be collecting views via classroom discussion, where many students will not contribute, meaning that the main views come from individuals with the confidence to share their opinions.

Student councils or student panels can help contextualise data you have gathered from all students, but they are of limited value when used in isolation. It is challenging to ensure that these groups are representative; the chances are they will provide their views and those of their close friends rather than those of the wider student body. When we look at perceptions of peer group behaviour, students are reasonably accurate in estimating how their close friends behave but often wildly inaccurate when describing their year group. The reasoning behind these assumptions is that most individuals think that others will behave worse than they do. Therefore, we can safely assume that a small cohort of students is unlikely to hold particularly accurate views about their peer group regarding behaviour or what is valued and relevant within PSHE without additional data sources to draw from.

Step 4 - PSHE programme plan

Your school will probably have a medium-term programme plan in place for PSHE. It will be self-evident if this plan has a balance of topics across the PSHE curriculum or if some subjects are taking up a lot of space. There may be good reasons for additional focus on some areas. For example, we know that, at a population level, smoking prevalence has been on a downward trajectory for many years. Most young people will not smoke, and we are quickly moving towards a 'smoke-free generation'. However, there are still pockets of significantly higher smoking rates. Schools situated in these areas will naturally wish to include more tobacco education in their PSHE programme compared with areas where there is very little or no smoking uptake.

If you have collected data from students, you will be able to adapt your programme according to needs, which will also be reflected in the shape of your PSHE curriculum. Of course, you will want to ensure that statutory requirements have been met; however, there will be areas where a lighter touch may be sufficient, leaving more time to focus on topics that need more attention.

The medium- and long-term planning of your PSHE programme should demonstrate that by age 16, students will have received comprehensive coverage of PSHE and will have had opportunities to acquire the knowledge, skills and values that enable them to develop the attributes and character that will help them navigate the next stage of education or training.

An effective PSHE programme will also have some flexibility. There are times when an issue arises that needs to be addressed quickly. This could be a national or even a global concern, such as a health epidemic or natural disaster, or something more localised, perhaps a tragedy affecting the school. In these instances, PSHE should focus on addressing the immediate needs.

A well-planned spiral, progressive curriculum will ensure essential learning is covered and allow topics to be revisited, avoiding the repetition that students are so critical of.

Figure 2.2 demonstrates how a topic can be developed across ages and stages to become more complex progressively, building up new information while creating opportunities to check prior learning. Each 'box' represents the content of a 2 hour pack of lesson activities, and there is no expectation that teachers will cover everything in each resource pack (Chameleon PDE, 2024). However, if the complete content of each were delivered, the approach taken would vary significantly, meaning that students would have a different learning experience each time the topic was revisited.

This approach encourages student curiosity and engagement, all supporting effective learning.

Step 5 – Check that they *really* know what they say they know!

Recognition of terminology does not equal understanding or even knowledge recall. Often, students recognise the title of a subject and assume that they 'already know' everything there is to know.

Ideally, you will want to be sure that students have knowledge about the topics covered and the skills to apply what they have learned. Over time, there should be an increased ability and confidence to make connections across and between PSHE subjects as learning develops and consolidates.

Students regularly report that they are knowledgeable about internet safety and that it has been covered effectively in school. However, data show that some students upload indecent images, and as they get older, the number engaging in this behaviour increases. So, are they 'really' sufficiently knowledgeable about internet safety? In a similar vein, students report that bullying is covered effectively, and although we see low levels of physical and online bullying being reported, experiences of verbal bullying are significantly higher. When it comes to reporting bullying, harassment or any other incidents where students feel unsafe, very high numbers report that they know where to report incidents; however, far fewer say that they would feel confident making a report.

You can take various steps to monitor progress, many of which can be built into lessons. Teachers frequently ask how they should assess PSHE, which is a complex question. The ambition of PSHE should always be to prepare students for managing

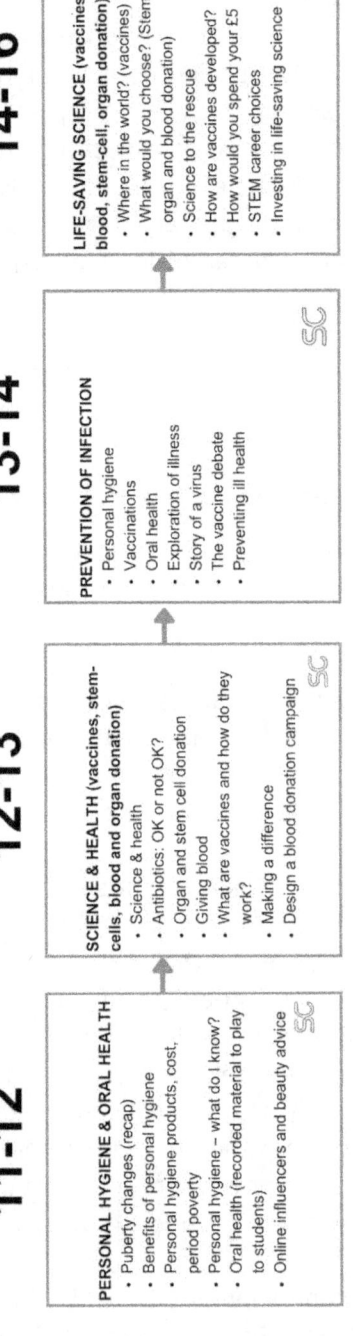

Figure 2.2 Example of progression of a topic across age range

life, relationships, choices, emotions, communication, values, and much more as effectively as possible. Many of these topics are nuanced, with no right or wrong answer or 'score' on how effectively a young person can do this. The knowledge part is easy to assess; however, as previously discussed, PSHE is much more than an accumulation of knowledge.

So, what should assessment look like?

Assessment in PSHE can be tricky as judgments are made about a student's personal qualities, values, knowledge and 'life skills'. However, if we are devoting precious curriculum time to this subject, it is reasonable to expect some form of measure as to whether learning has been effective. Assessment in PSHE lessons can be a valuable part of a school's Personal Development Education programme if it is planned and appropriate. It should also be used to improve the learning experience for students, leading to better educational outcomes.

It is generally accepted that ipsative assessment is a more realistic and useful approach with the added advantage of far less 'marking', saving teachers time.

Ipsative assessment is where a student considers their knowledge, skills, attitudes and values at the beginning of a lesson, topic, term or year, and then reflects on how these have changed owing to the teaching input. This places each pupil at the heart of the assessment process because the assessment is personalised and individual. This also removes the need for teachers to make judgements about students' personal characteristics or values and avoids measurement against arbitrary assessment statements (e.g. working towards, at, beyond), which may not suit every student.

This does not mean the teacher is a passive participant in this process, but we need to acknowledge that most teachers are not specialists in PSHE. Therefore, any assessment needs to be straightforward and expedient.

Figure 2.3 provies an example assessment model for PSHE. The model is based on the 6 term academic year in the UK, although the model works for any system or number of terms. Each half-term's assessment follows the same set pattern. This means that staff and students can quickly become familiar with the structure, while you can vary the content of the assessments, ensuring that they are diverse and exciting (Chameleon, 2024).

Students should have some format for recording their work, whether in a PSHE exercise book, folder, e-portfolio or whatever system your school uses. Note: fewer

	Introduce Learning Focus	Teacher provides a 3-minute overview of what's being covered this half-term.
	Baseline Assessment Part 1	A short learning task that allows the teacher to assess students' current knowledge, skills and understanding of the topic to be taught.
	Baseline Assessment Part 2	As the half-terms progress you will incorporate deep learning into the baseline assessment by asking students to reflect on prior learning.
	Teacher Assessment 1 No comments needed on student work	Collects student books/folders and makes a note of any misconceptions/questions that need addressing in this half-term. Reviews up-coming lessons and amends planning accordingly.
	End of Module Assessment-part 1	Students revisit the learning this half-term.
	End of Module Assessment-part 2	A deep learning activity that encourages students to make connections to other aspects of their personal development. In the last half-term of each year students complete an end of year review
	Teacher Assessment 2 Individual student comments	Collects student books/folders and writes an individual comment about each student's reflections. This does not have to be long, but should use positive language. They may also wish to suggest a formative target, again using a positive tone.

Figure 2.3 Assessment model for PSHE

assessment points should be included for students aged 15-16, as the last two half-terms of the school year will probably involve focused exam preparation, and PSHE may not be delivered.

Incorporating 'deeper' learning into PSHE

This model takes ipsative assessment one step further and incorporates elements of deep learning (Tait, 2020). Deep learning practices align with the spiral and progressive nature of PSHE education. This means that students can make stronger connections between different themes in your PSHE programme, their wider personal development and what they have learnt in PSHE from term to term and from year to year. They should also see its relevance and applicability to their lives, both now and in the future.

What about the perception of peer group behaviour?

A further area where students 'think' they know more than is often the case is how their peer group behaves. We shall return to this theme throughout this book.

Fortunately, most students make healthy and safe choices most of the time; however, it is widespread for students to overestimate the level of risk-taking in their peer group.

It is not only students who overestimate risk-taking behaviour; teachers and parents are also likely to adopt a more pessimistic view of teenage behaviour. An explanation for this may be our tendency to seek out information we already believe to be true. This is not surprising given the sensational headlines to which we are exposed on a regular basis. This can also lead to a lack of acceptance of evidence that contradicts firmly held beliefs.

This confirmation bias explains why anonymously collected data showing consistent results across a wide range of settings are sometimes challenged by students and staff, with the comment 'They must be lying', frequently shared. Of course, this makes no sense, as it would mean that students without knowledge of each other were lying in the same patterns across all the questions within a survey.

A long-term PSHE plan that includes anonymous student data collection can modify the programme to meet student needs and produce evidence of impact. Sharing this data with students further challenges them to acknowledge that what they 'think they know' is not always accurate.

KEY TAKEAWAYS

Acknowledge that students who consider a PSHE programme repetitive will be critical of lessons, and engagement and learning will be reduced.

Accept that students don't always 'know' as much as they think they do, and it is essential to have systems in place to establish a baseline for knowledge and skills.

Aspire to embed ipsative assessment with ambition for deep learning within your spiral, progressive PSHE programme.

PERSONAL REFLECTIONS

Use the space to make your own notes and reflections on this chapter.

1. Are there topics within your PSHE programme that are given significantly more time than others? Is there a rationale for the time allocated to different areas of the PSHE curriculum?

2. What are your perceptions about risk-taking behaviour within your student cohort? What evidence have you based this on?

3. How do you currently assess PSHE? Does your assessment model include deep learning?

FURTHER READING

Tait, J (2020) *Teaching Rebooted: Using the Science of Learning to Transform Classroom Practice*, Bloomsbury

LESSON PACK

Vaping, tobacco and cannabis – what you need to know

This lesson pack is a good example of the fast pace of change in PSHE. Just a few years ago, vaping was not something that we had to include within PSHE lessons; suddenly, it became the latest issue causing concern and a new topic to be addressed with students.

This lesson pack has been updated twice in the past few years to keep up with changes in legislation, and this will continue as further changes, and new research emerges.

The lesson pack includes quizzes to assess baseline knowledge, smoking prevalence worldwide, scenarios, a 'big tobacco' manipulation video and more. There are opportunities for discussion and assessment. There are over 2 hours of activities, and the session is designed for 12- to 13-year-olds.

RESOURCES

Assessment

Teachers often need help with assessment in PSHE. The ideas below provide a range of suggestions that you could use to provide evidence of student progress in healthy relationships.

The components of the assessment are:

- knowledge about healthy relationships;
- skills and values that support healthy relationships; and
- connected learning, which in turn provides evidence of deeper understanding.

Knowledge-based assessment – Healthy relationships

This short agree/disagree continuum is suitable for students aged 11–13. It could assess knowledge following lessons or as a baseline to ascertain existing knowledge. It also gives insight into your group's views and attitudes.

The agree/disagree activity checks knowledge and understanding, but also attitudes. These may differ from one group to the next, and by gaining insight, you will be able to target the areas that need more attention in the group you are working with.

The statements suggested can easily be adapted, and you can also use quizzes if assessing knowledge of legislation and other more fact-based learning. This is the easiest type of assessment; however, much of the content in PSHE requires a more nuanced approach to ascertain knowledge about less objective content; for example, what healthy relationships look like.

Ask students – Do you agree/disagree with the statements?

If space is available, students can place themselves on a continuum with agree at one end and disagree at the other. If sitting at a desk, they could write 'agree', 'disagree' or 'depends'. Take some feedback if offered from students.

1. A boyfriend/girlfriend will make someone feel happier.
2. Someone is too young for romance at 13.
3. If someone's friends are in a romantic relationship, they should be too.
4. Someone's girlfriend/boyfriend should be around the same age as them.

Copyright material from Angela Milliken-Tull (2025), *What Students Want From Their PSHE In Secondary School*, Routledge.

5. The legal age of sexual consent is 16 (in the UK) and should not be lowered.
6. Girls are usually ready for romantic relationships before boys as they are more mature.
7. If someone has a romantic partner, they have to kiss them.
8. Most students my age feel ready for a romantic relationship.
9. If a teenager has romantic feelings towards someone of the same gender they are definitely gay or bi-sexual.
10. Spending time with friends at this age is more fun than having a romantic relationship.

	Teacher follow-up questions/comments
1	What makes us happy? Is it ourselves or another person? Do we need to be happy all of the time? What's the difference between being happy and being contented?
2	Does everyone mature at the same rate? What do we mean by romance? Do romantic relationships always involve intimacy?
3	Can there be peer pressure to be in relationship? Do some teenagers put themselves under pressure to have a girlfriend/boyfriend?
4	What potential problems are associated with large age gaps, especially when one partner is young, e.g. under 16? What are the legal implications? What power balance issues may occur?
5	Should the age of sexual consent be increased?
6	In general girls do mature a little earlier than boys, but does this mean they are ready for romantic relationships? Or want them?
7	What do you know about consent?
8	Do some students say they are interested in a romantic relationship because they think it is what expected? Does society encourage this?
9	Why is it common for teenagers to feel confused about their feelings? (It's a time of discovering self-identity with lots of brain changes taking place, uncertainty is very common.)
10	Friendships are very important, why is it crucial to maintain friendships when you are involved in a romantic relationship?

Skills

Developing and practising skills is an integral part of PSHE and there are a range of options for monitoring progress in your group.

Below is an observation chart for healthy relationships lessons.

Note: the letters are a suggestion; you may wish to use ticks to indicate the observation level and leave boxes unfilled where skill has not been observed.

Student	Skills progress (C = consistent, M = mostly, N = not yet observed			
	Active listening	Negotiating	Respecting others	Presenting/giving feedback
1	C	N	C	N
2	N	N	N	N
3	C	C	C	N
4	N	N	N	M
5	M	M	M	C
6	M	N	C	C

Using Excel to update observations over a term will help provide evidence of your group's progress and indicate areas that may require additional focus.

PSHE lessons generally include opportunities for students to discuss scenarios or case studies, debate questions or suggest solutions. Within sessions, there should be a range of activities, such as paired discussion, group work and feedback on discussions, all of which can indicate how well students are developing various skills.

Observing students' interactions and updating your spreadsheet in real time will ensure an ongoing record of progress.

Individual reflections

It is essential for PSHE lessons to feel safe and to use distancing techniques as much as possible. However, there is also a place for individual reflection, allowing students to assess their progress and identify areas for improvement. This can be completed in a notebook, journal or online. The key is to ensure that this is confidential, with only teachers having access. You should comment occasionally and compare student reflections with your observations. However, you will not be displaying this work on open evenings.

You can provide students with a template to complete their reflections.

Term 3: Healthy relationships – Your reflections

The primary skills we focused on this term are listed below; add your reflections and comments.

Skills	Rate yourself on this skill. Good, OK, Difficult	How could you improve?	Teacher comments or initials
Active listening			
Negotiating			
Respecting others			
Presentation skills			

The teacher comments section may only be completed once per term, and comments may be made if required, such as if student reflections and teacher observations do not align.

Connected learning

A great way to test if your students have internalised the learning completed in PSHE is to ask them to demonstrate how a topic or theme they have been learning about links to other parts of the PSHE curriculum, the wider personal development curriculum or even the core curriculum. You can also include your school values as part of this assessment of how effectively your students are making the crucial connections that will evidence that their PSHE learning is becoming embedded in their deep learning.

A student logbook or journal is a great way to capture this, and ideally, you plan this to align with your PSHE programme with evidence of learning building as students move through the academic year and progress through the school.

A simple template can provide structure to this. Continuing the theme of healthy relationships, students can be challenged to make connections.

In PSHE you have been learning about *healthy relationships*. How has what you have learned connected to:	
Other topics in PSHE you have learned about earlier in the year	
Protected characteristics under the Equality Act 2010	
Something you have been learning about in other subjects	
Our school values	

3 Not another video, worksheet, quiz . . .
Injecting variety into PSHE lessons

Variety is the spice of life! This is something we should aim to apply in PSHE lessons. Not only will this keep sessions engaging and encourage student curiosity, but it will also ensure that different learning styles are accommodated. Feedback from students regarding the type of delivery style they prefer is, as expected, varied. Many enjoy discussion-based activities, while others prefer investigative tasks. Group work is popular, but some students favour individual work. Videos can present a wealth of information quickly and prompt discussion; case studies and scenarios help elicit how students will apply the knowledge they have learned. Quizzes are popular with all ages, particularly when it is a magazine-style quiz that presents personal insights. The accompanying lesson pack includes this style of quiz with a focus on how introverted or extroverted students are, based on the quiz results. Care should be taken to emphasise that these quizzes are not scientific!

The point here is that no one type of activity is the 'best' or 'worst' option, other than lecture style, which never goes down well. However, mixing activities makes lessons more interesting and more likely to keep students engaged.

Recently, there has been an increase in 'solutions' for PSHE lessons, generally involving an artificial intelligence (AI)-generated avatar or cartoon-style character presenting a video supported by a follow-up worksheet. This approach is marketed to teachers as a complete package, allowing them to sit back, relax, press a button and have their work done. This may sound tempting, and students may enjoy this approach initially. However, the repetitive style, character voice and predictability of the sessions will soon become tedious for both students and teachers. There is also a limited opportunity to explore and practise skills.

Despite the leaps in technology and the emergence of portal-based resources, unless the teacher can adapt and edit materials to meet students' needs, they can become cumbersome to use at best and potentially expensive, as well as largely redundant resources.

This is the case in all schools, particularly in special educational needs settings and international schools where some students may not have English as their first language. The ability to modify material, simplify language and break down lessons into small parts that can be delivered over several sessions or even a term is crucial for these schools. Within mainstream schools, it is also vital that materials can be adapted to ensure inclusivity and meet the needs of all students.

Top tips for introducing variety to PSHE lessons

- Don't be afraid to try something new; if it doesn't work, assess why and then modify it or don't do it again.

- If there's space to move around, include some activities such as standing in a continuum line according to a statement or reading and commenting on questions around the room. Dot voting, whereby the class reads different statements placed around the room, is another activity where students can get up from their desks to participate. This will help students who struggle with concentration to engage more effectively.

- Intersperse group work and paired activity with quieter independent tasks or reflections.

- Use different answering mechanisms for quizzes, e.g. continuum, moving to different corners for other answers, standing up, sitting down, thumbs up, etc. If technology is available, quizzes using programs such as Kahoot or Mentimeter can be fun and engaging. This will help assess progress.

- Give groups variations of the same problem, with each feeding back group findings to share learning.

- Use music, films and TV series as starters for discussions. This can be useful in lessons about relationships, and there is usually something popular in which many students are invested.

- Use short starter activities to baseline knowledge and build curiosity before moving on to longer tasks. The accompanying lesson pack includes three 10 minute activities.

- Give groups within the class different tasks to work on simultaneously. This allows you to differentiate activities according to students' needs. All groups will be able to provide feedback on their findings and share learning with the wider group.

- Consider more creative activities. These can help build self-worth and collaboration. For example, less structured activities in which students are tasked with creating an advisory booklet or poster for younger students, planning an event to fundraise or drafting a podcast discussion.

How will you know if the lesson is going well?

When trying new approaches in PSHE and potentially taking risks with your teaching, you will want to assess whether the session is going well. This is also an ideal opportunity to consider how effectively skills are being developed and practised. It's useful to have a mechanism for recording your observations and to include opportunities for students to reflect on their learning, including providing feedback on their skills development.

When learning is going well, it should be exciting and engaging and help students learn things they want to know. Students should experience a sense of belonging within their community and feel safe discussing the learning and sharing views.

Signs that learning is going well will include:

- Respect for each other will be demonstrated through active listening, good manners, taking turns, and 'agreeably disagreeing' where there are differences of opinion.
- Students will take risks and will be able to manage their emotions if things go wrong or if they make mistakes.
- There will be evidence of self-worth and empathy within the group.
- Collaboration will be evident, and students will enhance their understanding of what they need from other people and what they can offer to support others.
- There will be an increase in self-awareness as well as social awareness.

Knowledge, skills, values, attributes – getting the balance right

In education, there is a heavy bias towards the accumulation of knowledge, with schools and students rewarded for how successfully they have achieved this goal in the form of exam results. PSHE is not an examined subject, nor should it be, and this is a strength of the PSHE curriculum. There is still a focus on knowledge, but there is an opportunity to consider how this knowledge base melds with and supports skills, values and attributes, many of which will be expected by employers as knowledge becomes less valuable and skills more sought after.

This may sound counterintuitive, but think about the recent forward strides in research, medicine, translation and design driven by AI. No human can accumulate knowledge and apply it at the speed of machine learning. Therefore, skills that AI cannot replace, or those required to manipulate and work alongside AI, will become increasingly important in the future workforce. There will also be new jobs emerging that currently do not exist as we become increasingly immersed in ever more sophisticated technology in the workplace.

What do teachers want for their students?

When teachers are asked what 'gift' they would like their students to move on to the next stage of education with, they inevitably list skills and values, never knowledge. You can try this out with the teachers at your school. Give everyone a post-it note or gift card and ask them to write their suggestions.

Figure 3.1 provides some examples of the 'gifts' teachers have wished for their students.

A similar exercise tasks teachers with placing statements in a diamond 9 according to importance, with the most important statements at the top.

Give teachers a copy of the diamond 9 template (Figure 3.2) to complete the task. This task could also be used with students by placing 'I' before each statement.

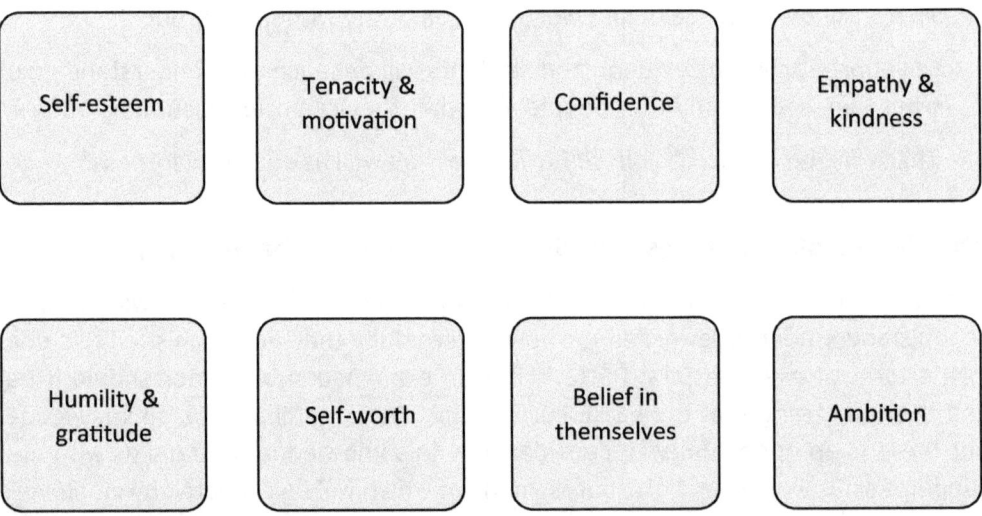

Figure 3.1 Find the connections activity

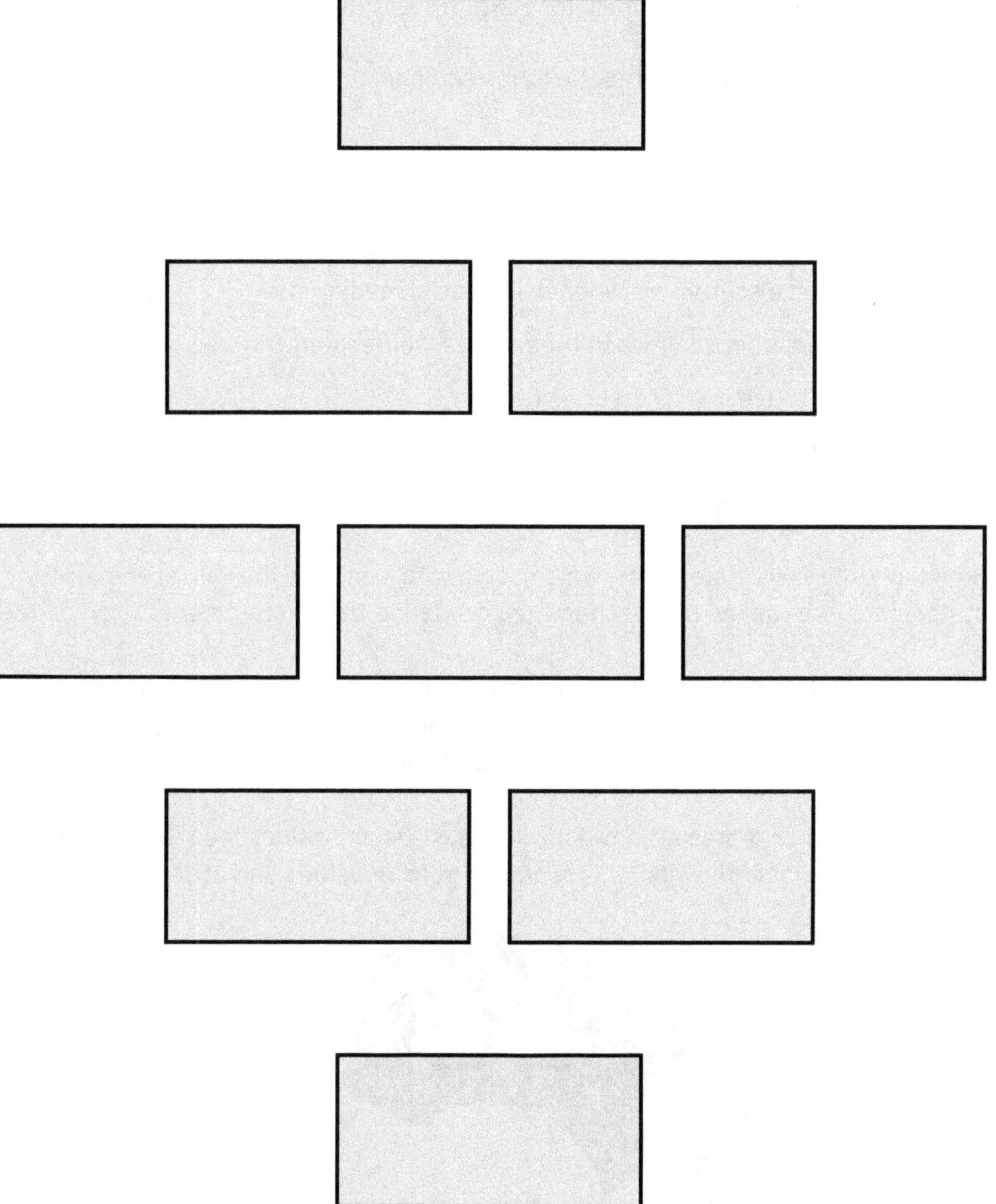

Figure 3.2 Diamond 9 Template

32 *What Students Want from their PSHE in Secondary School*

List the following nine 'outcomes' for PSHE (in a random order):

- Know that exercise benefits the lungs and heart
- Can resolve a conflict
- Describes what a safe and respectful community means to them
- Know there are different types of families
- Can act with discernment when using social media
- Identifies positive qualities in themselves (self-esteem)
- Can be assertive in a 'pressure situation'
- Reflects on own and others' values and beliefs
- Know the damaging effects of tobacco

Inevitably, the skills statements, which begin with 'can', and the values and attitudes statements, are ranked higher than the knowledge-based statements.

PSHE is an interplay between knowledge, skills, values, attitudes and attributes. A comprehensive programme offering a wide range of active learning opportunities will provide students with the chance to maximise their learning of all these components.

Figure 3.3 aims to represent how knowledge, skills and values feed into, inform and support each other. Knowledge is required to form values and attitudes, and skills

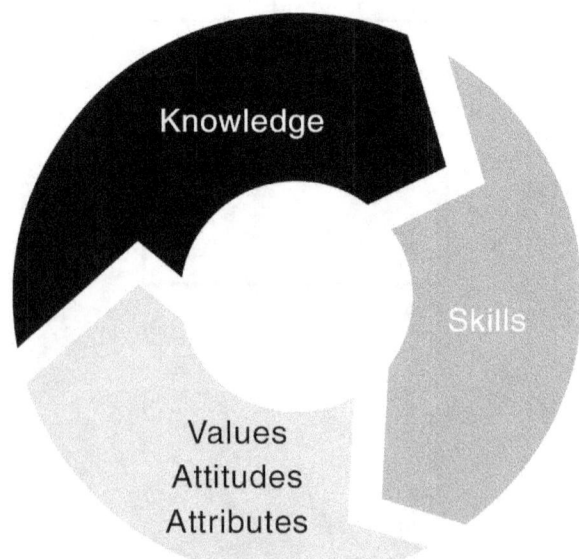

Figure 3.3 Interplay between knowledge, skills and attitudes

are necessary to apply knowledge and negotiate values and attitudes. For example, having been presented with knowledge input about alcohol, some students may decide that they do not wish to consume alcohol either now or in the future. This may be further backed by a value-based decision, e.g. their religion prohibits alcohol. However, this view will not be held by all of their peer group. Therefore, they need skills to acknowledge and accept values and attitudes different from their own and to be able to 'agreeably disagree'.

Social and emotional learning

It is probably becoming apparent that there are many opportunities within PSHE lessons to help students develop emotional intelligence or social and emotional learning (SEL). We are familiar with the concept of lifelong learning and continuous professional development, and this is an area that is becoming increasingly necessary as technology changes the workplace.

Social and emotional learning is a lifelong process that helps children succeed in school and, as adults, thrive in all aspects of life, including effective communication, building healthy and fulfilling relationships, regulating emotions, and managing challenges. This is implicit in an effective PSHE programme, but it can be useful to examine the key components within SEL.

You may have come across social and emotional learning (SEL) previously. It was popular for a few years, particularly in primary schools and with teachers. With government and funding changes, the initiative faded, but the fundamentals of SEL are as valid as they ever were.

Currently, the most renowned advocate of the SEL approach is CASEL (Collaborative for Academic, Social, and Emotional Learning). CASEL defines the five key aspects of SEL as follows:

Self-awareness is how we think about ourselves and who we are. It includes understanding our culture, thoughts and feelings, and what we believe we can achieve. It's also about understanding how these factors can influence our behaviour and beliefs.

Self-management is about managing our emotions, thoughts and actions as we work towards our goals. This includes coping with stress and anxiety, persevering through challenges and developing a sense of personal agency (a willingness and ability to take action to make a difference).

Social awareness is how we understand others, learn to take on different perspectives and have empathy for people, even those who are different from us.

It also includes understanding how what is happening around us can influence us and how we create and feel a sense of belonging.

Relationship skills are how we get along with others and how we form lasting friendships and connections. This includes communicating clearly, solving problems together, managing conflicts and disagreements, and standing up for ourselves and others.

Responsible decision-making involves making positive and informed choices. This includes considering the consequences of our actions, being curious and open-minded to new perspectives and information, and identifying solutions that benefit us and the community.

These descriptors sit very comfortably alongside the 'gifts' that teachers want to give their students, as well as the skills and values that take the top spots in the diamond 9 exercise.

Importantly, these skills are also essential if young people are to meet the criteria that employers are looking for as we move into a faster-paced change in the workplace, where adaptability and emotional intelligence are crucial. Figure 3.4 lists the top 10 skills that, according to the World Economic Forum (2023), employers currently need in workers.

Notably, six out of the 10 skills listed sit under 'self-efficacy' or ' working with others'. Emerging skills likely to increase in demand are listed below Figure 3.4.

Emerging skills
- AI and big data
- Systems thinking
- Talent management
- Service orientation and customer service

Other areas expected to be in demand are leadership and social influence, and life-long learning is likely to be essential for everyone. It is estimated that six in 10 workers in the current workforce will need to be trained to keep up with changing jobs.

The value of active learning and emotional intelligence – Academic prowess is not enough!

For 10 years, I worked with academic students set on engineering, science or technology careers. The students had deferred places to top universities and had

Ranking	Cognitive skills
1	Analytical thinking
2	Creative thinking
	Self-efficacy
3	Resilience, flexibility, agility
4	Motivation and self-awareness
5	Curiosity and life-long learning
7	Dependability and attention to detail
	Technology skills
6	Technological literacy
	Working with others
8	Empathy and active listening
9	Leadership and social influence
	Management skills
10	Quality control

Figure 3.4 Top skills employers are looking for

opted for a work-based gap year before commencing their studies. My role was to manage the team supporting this group of students and liaise with employers, and I also oversaw the training that students completed during their work placement. There were two components of this training: the first was a technical project, and the second was an introductory management qualification.

Future leaders need a suite of skills

Employers recognised that academic ability alone would not be enough to prepare future 'captains of industry', and the majority were very supportive of the less technical side of the training expectations. Students didn't always embrace this aspect of their gap year experience quite so enthusiastically!

The training course commenced before the work placement. Over a few days, the group got to know each other, completed team-building exercises, and were introduced to basic information about managing workload, communication with colleagues, time-keeping and the softer skills that they would be developing and logging over the course of the coming months. Two further one-day sessions throughout the year focused on interpersonal skills via active learning activities. Students were required to build a portfolio of tasks and reflections, which would be assessed. If all criteria were met and agreed with their workplace supervisor, a qualification was awarded.

Sometimes 'young dogs' don't want to learn new tricks!

The teaching and learning style employed in the training sessions was alien to this group. Most had completed only maths and science A levels, although many were highly accomplished in various academic endeavours; some were musically proficient and others had been engaged in competitive sports. A significant number of students had also completed the Duke of Edinburgh award. However, some had been entirely focused on academic achievement to the exclusion of everything else, and this group tended to take exception to completing a more 'vocational' type of qualification.

'I'm too clever for this!'

The main complaint was that it was 'a waste of time'; they resented the perceived low value of the qualification. It was roughly equivalent to an A level, but no exam existed. The students felt that they were 'too clever' to be bothered with this type of qualification; they would, after all, be taking up their place at Cambridge or some other prestigious university following their gap year. Only a handful of the 100-plus group did not complete the qualification. As the year continued, most who had been initially sceptical came to appreciate the benefits of the training.

Where it all went wrong

However, two 'refusers' fell foul of their responsibilities in the workplace, and one had his contract terminated. The other young man had proved challenging during the initial training session. He was rude to other students while thinking he was being humorous, difficult in group work and very childish and irritating. The group quickly started avoiding him and tutors spent lots of time trying to reintegrate him into the group.

During his placement, a serious incident occurred where, following weeks, if not months of inappropriate behaviour and comments towards colleagues, many of which included sexualised content, he became the victim of a 'prank' by the all male group. Instead of pursuing more formal routes to complain about the situation, they took it into their own hands and tied him to a chair. The outcome was that the student was moved to an environment where a senior staff member supervised him and he was always accompanied for the remainder of his work placement. The colleagues involved in the prank received a final written warning.

What can we learn from this?

The moral of this tale is that academic prowess does not guarantee, or even suggest, that an individual will be successful in the workplace. The skills associated with social and emotional learning are crucial, and teachers are in an ideal position to support this, with PSHE lessons providing the perfect environment.

CASE STUDY

Active teaching and learning methods in PSHE

Joanna Feast | Independent education consultant specialising in PSHE and wellbeing

Active teaching and learning is when learners are at the heart of the lesson and participate meaningfully. They can assimilate and accommodate their learning into their pre-existing knowledge and skill development to see if they can make further progress. There is space to be curious, ask questions and manipulate information to become motivating and highly relevant.

One of the most important aspects of effective PSHE lessons is that pupils feel physically and psychologically safe to participate. Teachers must hold firm that pupil safety is paramount and cannot compromise this at the expense of a supposedly exciting or innovative method. It is important to remember that what might appear to be an 'engaging' task for some pupils can be uncomfortable for others, so methods need to be 'low-stakes', regardless of the topic at hand. All PSHE lessons must include a group agreement or ground rules that feature the right to pass, so pupils do not have to participate in an activity if they don't want to.

Any active teaching and learning method needs to encourage the advocacy of pupils; methods need to show congruence between instructions, the task itself and how it is assessed. In PSHE, providing a range of stimulating opportunities/ experiences for depth and breadth of learning is fundamental. And it is really important that there is no 'ceiling' of achievement or progression.

Where to start? The most effective PSHE lessons begin with identifying where pupils are currently, then considering how they can progress, and selecting tasks that support, enable and empower this development. Tasks must be age and stage appropriate, high quality and based on skill development.

It is a good idea to select active teaching and learning methods that offer two roles in one, firstly, to facilitate effective learning and secondly, to assess learning – so a task can be performed at the beginning and end of a topic to note progress. Some examples include:

• Diamond 9	• Ask-it basket
• Team challenges	• Group work
• Thought shower	• Think, pair, share
• Mingle bingo	• Draw and write/projective techniques
• Quizzes (limit use of true/false)	• Distanced scenarios – written or acted out, with puppets/characters (SEN/primary schools)
• Graffiti wall	
• Card sort	• Ranking attitudes
• Debate	• Mind map
• Role-play (if students enjoy this!)	• Hot topic interviews
• Attitude continuum statements	• Questionnaire/survey
• Carousel	
• Stem sentences	

A common feature of active teaching and learning methods is that they promote creativity and don't necessarily have a 'right' answer. This is wholly appropriate for PSHE as learning about life skills in the real world often means that nuance must be considered.

Finally, it is vital to employ a variety of methods to keep PSHE lessons relevant, intriguing and effective.

KEY TAKEAWAYS

Acknowledge that teachers are perfectly placed to support the social and emotional learning that will benefit many aspects of life, and active learning methods help enable this.

Accept that there is no one best 'solution' for delivering PSHE and a variety of teaching strategies will provide variety, encourage curiosity and engage with different learning styles

Aspire to create PSHE lessons that balance knowledge, skill, values and attitudes and prepare students for the qualities that employers will value.

PERSONAL REFLECTIONS

Use the space below for your comments and reflections about this chapter.

1. Which active teaching methods do you currently use when delivering PSHE sessions? Have you noticed activities that engage students more/less?

2. Do your PSHE sessions support social and emotional learning? Do you agree with the benefits associated with this approach?

3. Can PSHE sessions play a more active role in preparing students for work? How does your school link PSHE and career education within the wider personal development curriculum?

FURTHER READING

CASEL (2024) Collaborative for Academic, Social, and Emotional Learning, https://casel.org/

Alice Hoyle & Esther McGeeney (2020) *Great Relationships and Sex Education200+ Activities for Educators Working with Young People* (Routledge)

RESOURCES

Variety

There are many ways to inject variety into your lessons, and students often enjoy short quizzes and challenges. These can be used as starter activities or when time is limited, such as tutor time.

Although the aim is to provide short, enjoyable activities, these can also provide evidence of progress, and it is helpful to note how successfully classes complete the challenges. They lend themselves well to paired or group work, which offers opportunities to observe student interactions. Reminding students of the agreed ground rules before commencing these tasks is always advisable.

You can take inspiration from the types of quizzes and puzzles popular online. However, for inclusivity, the examples below are 'low-tech' and can be completed without a mobile phone or computer access.

The starter activity examples can be modified for different age groups, and it would be more useful if they tied in with the theme covered in PSHE. There are also opportunities to build general knowledge-type questions in the clues or information from other curriculum areas.

The themes in the examples are bullying, respect, diversity and the environment

Starter/tutor time activity 1 – Can you find the connections?

This is based on the *New York Times* quiz. The more challenging option contains 16 words, and the aim is to group them into sets of four, all connected somehow. The easier option has nine words with four sets of three connected words.

The jumbled words would be displayed on a whiteboard or students could be given a photocopy of the words. They would then work in pairs or teams to find the connections.

You can move around the class, giving clues. For example, if students have selected four words, you can tell them if they are correct, if three of the four are connected, etc.

Not another video, worksheet, quiz... 41

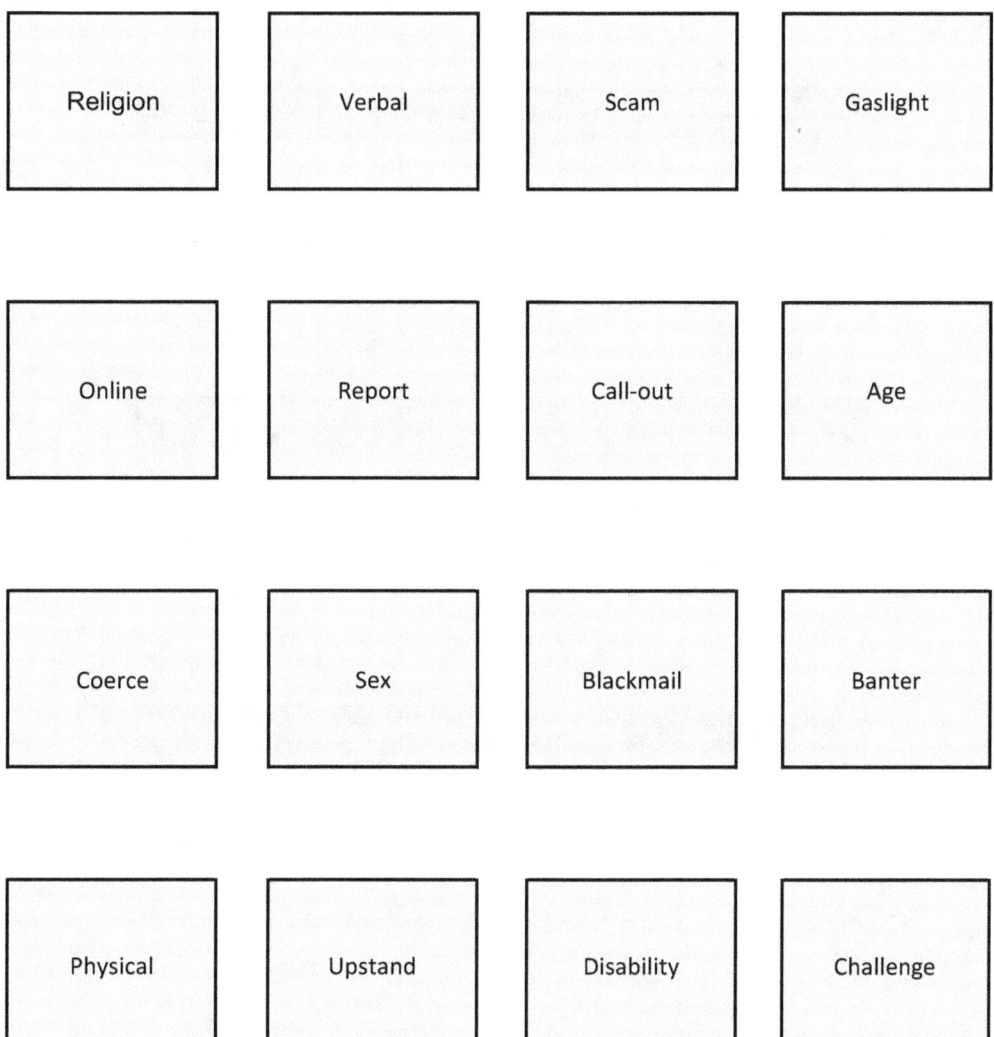

If the activity takes too long, you can reveal one of the connections.

To simplify the task, remove one word from each group to create a 3 × 4 grid, or remove a group entirely, making a 3 × 3 grid.

Answers

Protected Characteristics – Equality Act 2010

| Religion | Age | Sex | Disability |

Types of bullying

| Verbal | Online | Physical | Banter |

Misuse or abuse of power

| Scam | Coerce | Blackmail | Gaslight |

Actions that can be taken against bullying

| Report | Upstand | Call-out | Challenge |

Activity 2 - Find the word activity

Students are given a set of questions to answer, and the first letter of each is used to find a word, i.e. something related to what you have been covering in PSHE.

It will be more challenging if the letters from the clues that will form the word are not in order. Students will need to arrange the letters to form the correct word.

The word being searched for is

DIVERSITY

Clues:

1. What you pay when you borrow money (or earn if you save)
2. There are 12 months in this
3. Companies pay this to shareholders
4. Energy from the sun
5. A species that is becoming rarer is said to be this
6. A clever person can be described as this
7. Someone who doesn't eat meat
8. Dreadlocks are associated with this group
9. Police forces that work across many countries

> Rearrange the first letter of each clue to find the word

Answers

1. Interest
2. Year
3. Dividend
4. Solar

Copyright material from Angela Milliken-Tull (2025), *What Students Want From Their PSHE In Secondary School*, Routledge.

5. Endangered
6. Intelligent
7. Vegetarian
8. Rastafarian
9. Interpol

If this is too challenging, you can help by giving one or two letters as they appear in the word.

_ _ _ E _ _ _ T _

Activity 3 – Word search

This activity can be completed individually or in pairs and easily facilitated. The level of challenge can be set by providing only a grid or including the words within the grid.

Including crucial vocabulary that will be discussed and developed in the lesson or that should be familiar from work that has already been covered can turn this activity into a simple assessment of progress.

ENVIRONMENT WORD SEARCH

Find the hidden words linked to the environment

Can you find the 12 hidden words?

ENVIRONMENT WORD SEARCH

Find the hidden words linked to the environment

B	E	C	O	S	Y	S	T	E	M	A	T	I	C	S
I	C	G	G	R	E	E	N	H	O	U	S	E	A	U
O	O	Y	R	E	N	V	L	E	R	R	E	N	R	S
D	L	U	E	P	P	I	D	R	R	P	N	V	P	T
I	O	D	W	R	T	P	L	G	E	A	E	I	A	A
V	G	S	S	F	L	R	T	R	N	T	R	R	R	I
E	I	O	S	E	E	O	F	T	E	T	G	O	T	N
R	C	L	T	N	A	T	E	A	W	Y	Y	M	Y	A
S	A	A	L	E	P	E	A	S	A	I	E	E	T	B
I	L	R	A	W	I	C	O	E	B	I	F	N	I	I
T	F	P	C	A	C	T	O	V	I	A	F	T	A	L
Y	E	A	Y	B	P	I	L	A	L	E	I	A	G	I
C	F	N	C	L	C	O	C	C	I	M	C	L	S	T
A	E	E	Y	E	C	N	F	R	T	E	I	I	L	Y
T	F	L	C	L	C	L	F	C	Y	M	E	S	S	T
I	E	I	Y	G	C	A	F	W	I	D	N	T	O	Y
O	E	S	P	O	L	L	U	T	A	N	T	D	L	Y
N	E	T	O	E	C	O	F	R	I	E	N	D	L	Y

PROTECTION   ECOLOGICAL   POLLUTANT   RENEWABILITY

SUSTAINABILITY   ECOSYSTEM   GREENHOUSE   SOLAR PANEL

ENERGY-EFFICIENT   ENVIRONMENTALIST   ECO-FRIENDLY   BIODIVERSITY

Copyright material from Angela Milliken-Tull (2025), *What Students Want From Their PSHE In Secondary School*, Routledge.

Not another video, worksheet, quiz ... 47

ENVIRONMENT WORD SEARCH

Answer Key

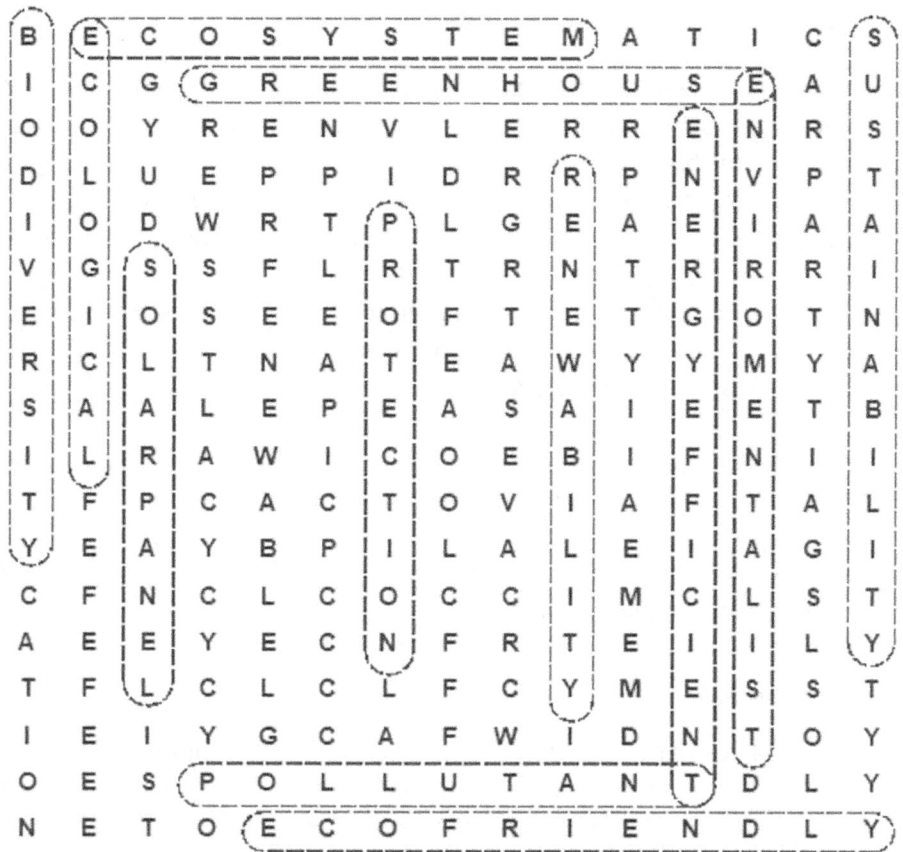

PROTECTION   ECOLOGICAL   POLLUTANT   RENEWABILITY

SUSTAINABILITY   ECOSYSTEMATIC   GREENHOUSE   SOLAR PANEL

ENERGY-EFFICIENT   ENVIRONMENTALIST   ECO-FRIENDLY   BIODIVERSITY

Copyright material from Angela Milliken-Tull (2025), *What Students Want From Their PSHE In Secondary School*, Routledge.

4 We are uniquely transient
A brief introduction to the amazing teenage brain

How often have we heard parents say that their child left home in the morning to start secondary school and returned a completely different person? Despite the exaggeration of this statement, there is no doubt that children undergo many changes in the few years from leaving primary school to the end of secondary school, and this can be a difficult time for children, parents and teachers to navigate.

Adolescence is between childhood and adulthood and lasts between the ages of 10 and 24 years. It is when individuals develop their sense of self and identity and will increasingly care about how others see them.

So, what is happening? What has changed a relaxed, mild-mannered, compliant child into an argumentative, grumpy, emotional adolescent?

A few factors contribute to these changes, but the most significant are changing hormone levels and brain development.

Brain development

The teenage brain goes through a period of transformation that makes it unique in that it is not a bigger version of a younger child's brain nor a smaller version of an adult brain. It is undergoing a process of pruning connections that are no longer needed. New pathways are developed that are more efficient and communicate better. The areas of the brain responsible for social experiences change, and this can lead to a greater focus on peer relationships. Reactions to stress may change, and mental health issues can arise for some.

While this is happening, there are some marvellous advantages, including:

- Development of complex thinking processes
- Creativity and abstract thinking

- Ability to adapt and take on new challenges
- Being poised to develop resilience

However, there are also some vulnerabilities associated with teenage brain development, including:

- Potential for stress to develop into stress-related illnesses such as anxiety or depression
- Needing more sleep – brain development is exhausting, and lack of sleep can make it more challenging to manage changes
- Difficulty controlling impulses, which can lead to poor decision-making, including accidents
- Greater susceptibility to the effects of substances such as tobacco/nicotine and alcohol.

It is interesting to note that many individuals who have mental health illnesses as adults will report that their first episode of mental ill health was experienced in adolescence.

Understanding why teenagers act the way they do and how to support them

Teachers and parents will want to encourage young people to make the most of their greater learning capacity. However, increasing independence and a growing propensity to challenge adults can make this difficult. Nonetheless, as adults, we should aim to understand the changes they are experiencing rather than fight against them. The lesson pack accompanying this chapter provides 2 hours of activities looking at what affects mental health. Included in this pack is a short video looking at teenage brain development.

We can also help young people understand and manage the vulnerabilities that are so common at this time. Young people feel things more intensely, resulting in more extreme emotions. Risk-taking increases as the area of the brain that understands and foresees consequences is under 'construction'. Sleep patterns also tend to change at this time, with adolescents needing more sleep but falling asleep later and feeling very tired and not adequately rested when they get up to arrive at school on time.

There have been calls over the years to change the school day to accommodate this, but in most places, the school day remains as it has always been, with an early start that does not take account of the natural sleep pattern changes that teenagers experience.

Inadequate sleep can negatively impact anyone, but possibly affect teenagers even more adversely!

Hormones

Alongside rapid brain development, adolescents also experience hormone fluctuations as they enter and progress through puberty. Adrenal stress hormones, sex hormones and growth hormones are all produced in greater quantities and can influence brain development. In boys, testosterone production increases 10-fold, and girls experience fluctuations of reproductive hormones that can significantly impact mood.

The physical side of puberty receives much attention, as it should. However, many emotional changes are taking place at this time, and these account for many of the reactions and difficulties in managing emotions that young people experience as they enter their teenage years. It is vital to acknowledge and support emotional as well as physical changes.

Everyone has an individual journey through adolescence; for some, it will be far more plain sailing than for others. Nonetheless, it is fair to say that it is rare for a young person to have a completely smooth transition from childhood to early adulthood.

The quote later in this chapter taken from a teenager's diary in 1969 also demonstrates that self-absorption has long been a mainstay of teenage life, with historical events appearing as a footnote! (Blackmore, 2019)

Peer influence

A further, far less tangible factor that we need to consider during this uniquely transient period is the influence of peers. Where younger children look to adults, most notably parents, grandparents or teachers, for approval, teenagers are far more interested in the views of their peers. Given the fact that they are all experiencing a melting pot of hormone and brain changes, this 'peer approval' can be both complex and unreliable; add in the pervasive world of social media, and we have a time bomb ready to explode at any moment.

Alongside a growing need for independence and experimentation, adolescents try to work out who they are. Throughout the teenage years, there may be periods of 'reinventing' themselves as they potentially move across and between different peer groups. Some may be questioning their sexuality, gender or both. Crushes and infatuations, which can be all-consuming for some young people, may be experienced, and many will be riding a tidal wave of emotions at some point during this tumultuous time.

For most, things eventually calm down as hormones settle and the period of rapid brain development slows. Many will show signs of maturity by their mid to late teens, but it can take longer for others. Peak brain development and hormone overdrive for many will be between 12 and 15. Girls generally enter this phase a little earlier and boys a little later.

How 'risky' are the teenage years?

As mentioned earlier, the developing teenage brain is more open to taking risks and less sensitive to consequences. Experimentation with clothing, make-up, hobbies and less innocent rites of passage occurs. This perpetuates commonly held misperceptions that teenagers are wild party animals, regularly use substances and have underage sex. This is very far from the truth, as the charts in Figure 4.1 demonstrate. The reality is that most young people do not engage in high-risk behaviour, although the numbers do rise as they get older.

There are often wide gaps between perceptions of substance use and what is happening. Very few young people smoke in the UK, and although vaping has increased, the majority do not vape. The incidence of alcohol use is a little higher but still significantly lower than perceptions, and cannabis use is low and has remained at similar rates over many years.

Figure 4.1 (Chameleon 2024) demonstrates substance use in different age groups across two academic years. A wide gap exists between the perception of peer group behaviour and actual behaviour. Interestingly, vaping, which has received a lot of media attention in recent years, provides the most significant gap between perception and reality.

Cannabis use in both younger people and the adult population has been very stable for several years, but there is often a perception that it is widely used amongst secondary school age students.

What can teachers do to support the needs of a 'uniquely transient 'cohort?

Be patient

First and foremost, it is essential to understand and have patience with students during this time, despite the challenges this may present. PSHE, or health and wellbeing lessons, offer opportunities to discuss and explore the issues students may be experiencing in a safe environment. This can only happen if there are timetabled sessions and teachers feel adequately equipped to deliver high-quality content in lessons and tutor groups effectively.

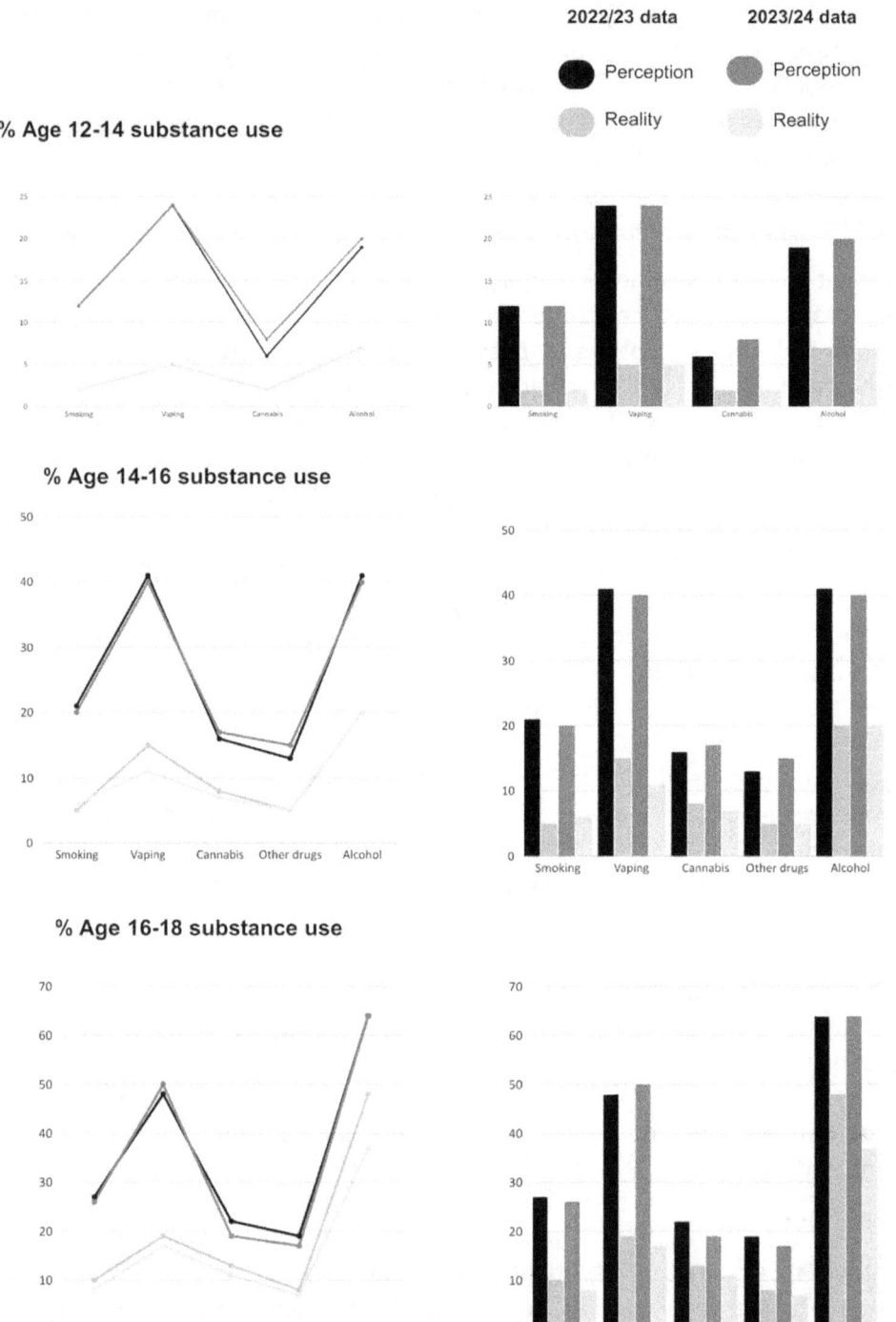

Figure 4.1 Substance use in different age groups of secondary school students. Comparision over 2022/23 and 2023/24 academic year

Be positive

Maintaining a focus on the positive behaviour choices that most students make most of the time can go a long way towards encouraging ongoing 'healthy' options at a time when students are naturally more predisposed to risk-taking. Simply knowing that most of their peers are *not* partaking in a behaviour widely perceived as commonplace can be protective. After all, if peer approval is so crucial during this phase of adolescence, why would a young person choose to do something that the peer group are not?

Be adaptive

Adapting lessons to the group's needs and avoiding a 'one size fits all' approach will help ensure that content is relevant to your students. This is where data collection, both quantitative and qualitative, can provide insights that allow PSHE leads to plan a programme that focuses on what will benefit students the most rather than delivering a prescribed set of lessons that may lack relevance, which in turn will lead to disgruntled students who feel misunderstood.

Be factual

Students must understand the safety and legal implications as they become increasingly independent and consider engaging in exploratory behaviour. Providing facts about this is relatively straightforward; however, a more subtle approach that can support harm reduction is to make students aware of the actual figures around a range of behaviours. This works best when you have collected data from your students.

Be understanding

It can be difficult for young people to manage their emotions during this time and as an influential and possibly trusted adult in their lives it is important to try and show kindness, care and understanding. This can be challenging, but as adults we have already come through the turmoil of the teenage years and are in a far stonger and more stable position with the maturity and experience that enables us to manage our own emotions far more effectively. Therefore we are in a good position to support the young people we encounter.

We should also be aware of adolescents' intense internal focus on what is currently going on in their lives, often to the exclusion of everything else. A letter to the *Guardian* newspaper provides an excellent example of this and demonstrates that nothing much has changed throughout the decades.

I went to arts centre (by myself!) in yellow cords and blouse. Ian was there but he didn't speak to me. Got rhyme put in my handbag by someone who's apparently got a crush on me. It's Nicholas I think. UGH!

Man landed on moon. (Teenage diary entry, 20 July 1969. From a letter sent to *The Guardian;* Blackmore, 2019)

CASE STUDY
Supporting change Emma Breeze, Senior leader, SEEAT

We are uniquely transient. (In the words of a teacher)

As I look at my own small children, just embarking on their educational careers, and my year 13s on the brink of moving on to university and work, I can't help but feel philosophical about the astronomical changes that occur over a child's time at school.

I've been lucky enough to work across primary and secondary settings over the last 16 years. The key similarity is the amount of change students go through over the course of their school careers. I would go so far as to say this is one of the greatest joys of being a teacher: seeing your students evolve and change in terms of their studies and also their move towards adulthood.

We have all encountered children who go through massive changes throughout their school careers – some undoubtedly more extreme than others. The student who was a little tearaway becomes a reformed character. The shy and quiet child flourishes and becomes more confident. The student who goes through something complicated outside of school, who, with the nurture and support of the school community, comes through the other side. These are extremes, but all children we encounter undergo their versions of these journeys as they develop into their adult selves. (Indeed, into adulthood and beyond!)

PSHE is essential to this journey – supporting students to see that who they are is not set in stone but constantly evolving. Giving them a safe place to discuss and learn the information is critical to understanding what is happening to them as they grow. It's a powerful subject. Talking to my sixth form students, they look back on their younger selves with nostalgia and surprise – charting their own journeys and evolutions. As they go on to life after school, they leave with the knowledge that they can change their character and life is not set: they are uniquely transient.

KEY TAKEAWAYS

Acknowledge that most young people do not regularly engage in high-risk behaviour, and by sharing this knowledge with them, you are encouraging positive social norms.

Accept that adolescence is a uniquely transient time for young people. You, as a teacher, are a trusted adult in a position to support them through this turbulent time with the knowledge and strategies that will help them become resilient young adults.

Aspire to deliver a PSHE programme based on the needs of students in your setting that is adaptive, inclusive, regularly reviewed, and updated.

PERSONAL REFLECTIONS

1. Do you have data to accurately inform you about the students' perceptions, behaviour and views in your setting? If yes, could this be improved?
2. Are any areas or topics within your PSHE programme covered too much or too little? Where are the gaps? How do you know?
3. Is it essential for teachers to know more about teenage brain development? How can PSHE support students through this complex phase of growth?

FURTHER READING

If you would like to learn more about adolescent brain development, a leading expert is Professor Sarah-Jayne Blackmore. The links below are to two of her talks that are available on You Tube

Blackmore S, Ted Talk, https://www.youtube.com/watch?v=6zVS8HIPUng (this was recorded in 2012, but is still useful).

The Neuroscience of the Teenage Brain (2019), https://www.youtube.com/watch?v=yQXhFa8dRCI

Blackmore S (2019) *Inventing Ourselves, The Secret Life of the Teenage Brain* (Black Swan)

Dwek CS (2017) *Mindset, Changing the Way you Think to Fulfil Your Potential* (Robinson Publishing)

Hohnen B, Gilmour J and Murphy T (2019) *The Incredible Teenage Brain: Everything You Need to Know to Unlock Your Teen's Potential* (JKB)

LESSON PACK

Quite a few lessons would fit comfortably within this chapter, including managing peer approval, sleep and relaxation, and even physical and emotional changes at puberty.

However, perhaps the most helpful lesson pack that will provide a foundation and scaffold for other topics is 'What affects mental health'. This lesson pack offers a range of activities that consider mental health issues, some common triggers and strategies to help young people understand and manage minor emotional difficulties. A short video provides a simple overview of teenage brain development.

We are uniquely transient 57

RESOURCES

Managing strong emotions

Teenagers feel emotions strongly. Whether it's anger, excitement, grief, embarrassment, or love, the chances are that their reactions will be more extreme than those of adults.

The following activities will suggest some strategies that students can use to help manage their feelings when emotions are elevated and there is also an opportunity to consider how they can advise or support someone experiencing a highly emotional situation.

The case studies are designed for different age groups; some more appropriate for younger students. Each recommends the age group it is most suitable for.

Remember to share the ground rules before starting the activities.

Activity 1 - What makes emotions run high? (20 minutes)

This activity is designed to acknowledge and identify the emotions that can be difficult for students to manage, may trigger an outburst or feel overwhelming.

Write the suggestions below on a piece of paper and place around the classroom. Students should then walk around and place a dot on the three they find the most emotionally challenging. They can use a pen or sticky dots to make their choices.

Please add to or change the suggestions.

> Being left out
>
> Being laughed at
>
> Someone talking about you behind your back
>
> Ignored by someone you like
>
> Embarrassed in front of friends
>
> Someone you like talking to you
>
> Made to feel stupid
>
> Unflattering photos posted on social media
>
> Rude comments on social media
>
> Parents being strict/controlling

Copyright material from Angela Milliken-Tull (2025), *What Students Want From Their PSHE In Secondary School*, Routledge.

Share the top three with the class and ask the group to identify the physical responses to the situations described. If your class is confident, they can discuss this in pairs and feed back suggestions. Otherwise, they can work individually, and the teacher can give feedback, having moved around the group to note the commonly occurring themes.

Physical responses to high emotions

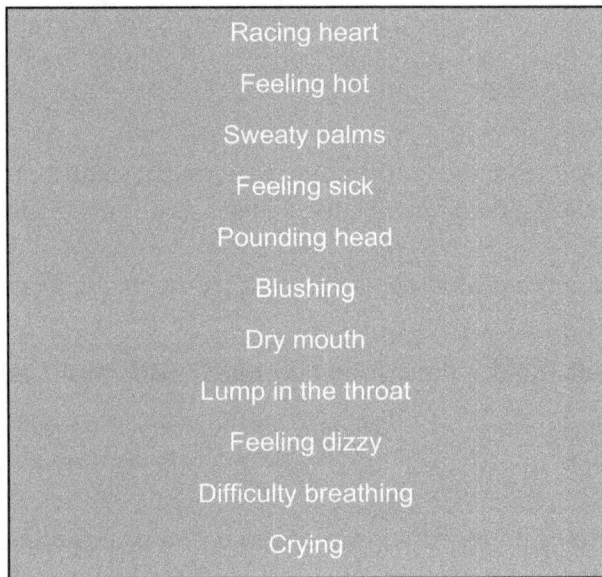

Racing heart
Feeling hot
Sweaty palms
Feeling sick
Pounding head
Blushing
Dry mouth
Lump in the throat
Feeling dizzy
Difficulty breathing
Crying

Not everyone will experience all these physical symptoms, but they will probably be familiar with some. All are synonymous with the fight-flight-freeze response that occurs when the body is under stress, either physically or emotionally.

The next part of the activity involves asking students to suggest some things they can do when emotions are running high to feel more under control.

What can be done to help calm emotions?

Give a few minutes for discussion in small groups or pairs and take some feedback. Share the information in the table with the class.

	Immediate responses
1	*Breathing.* Taking deep, slow breaths where you breath in for a count of four and then breath out for a count of eight slows heartbeat, reduces blood pressure and allows your brain to function better. This allows your emotional state to become rational again.
2	*Distraction.* Focus on a body sensation such as how the chair feels you are sitting on or look around the room to find objects of a particular colour. By taking your focus away from the thing that has caused high emotions you allow yourself an opportunity to settle and refocus.
3	*Words.* Tell yourself how you are feeling. This is called emotional labelling and research has shown that by using words to describe how you are feeling the emotional response is reduced and you are less likely to respond in a way you might regret. For example, if you see a post on social media that is insulting ask yourself how it makes you feel, e.g. I feel hurt, insulted and angry. Labelling your feelings makes you less likely to act irrationally.

Ask the groups to discuss any techniques they know about that can help regulate and process emotions. Take some feedback and then share the information in the table. Did the group include these?

	Longer term strategies
1	*Exercise.* For many, exercise is a good way to manage emotions. It makes us focus on physical sensations such as breathing harder. There can also be concentration involved in many sports. Being part of a team or group can be beneficial, and the release of endorphins can also help us feel more positive.
2	*Mindfulness or meditation.* Being present in the moment, aware of thoughts but not reacting to them and controlling breathing can all help with emotional regulation. There are lots of apps to support this and with practice many find it very beneficial.
3	*Journaling.* Writing down thoughts and feelings can help with processing them and give perspective. Including gratitude within journaling also helps with emotional regulation, e.g. three things I'm grateful for today are …

There is more to positive psychology than the suggestions provided. However, this is a good starting point and relatively straightforward to remember.

Conclude this activity by asking students to write down three things they are grateful for. Explain that these should be simple everyday gratitudes.

Activity 2 – Emotional turmoil, what would you advise? (20 minutes)

This activity considers some of the highly emotional situations that teenagers may experience. Using distanced techniques keeps the learning safer and less personalised.

Three scenarios are used to depict emotionally charged situations. Working in groups, the class is tasked with advising the individual or individuals in the scenario.

Scenario 1 – The heartbreak after the summer romance (suitable for age 12+)

Lena had always believed in the idea of love at first sight. It had happened one warm summer evening at a bonfire party at the end of the summer term. It was a beautiful, warm night with a full moon. She had been there with friends, laughing and chatting when Noah arrived. He had joined the school a few months previously, and something about him made Lena's heart race. They talked for hours, the way two people do when they feel an instant connection, and by the end of the night, Noah had kissed her under the stars, and they made plans to meet up the next day.

That was 4 months ago.

Now, as Lena sat in her room on a chilly November afternoon, staring at the unopened text from Noah on her phone, she couldn't help but replay the events in her mind, trying to understand how everything had gone wrong.

At first, things had felt perfect. They'd spent the entire summer together, going to concerts, meeting most days, and discussing their dreams, fears and hopes for the future. It felt like they were the only two people who understood each other. But as the school year started, everything shifted. Noah had grown distant; his responses to her texts became slower, and he began making excuses not to hang out. Then came the breakup message, short and cold: 'I think we should end things. I need space. I hope you understand.'

Lena didn't understand. She had been blindsided, devastated. She spent the next few days in a haze, hardly able to function. The mornings felt impossible without seeing Noah's name on her phone or hearing his laugh echoing in her mind. She had tried to reach out, sending messages that went unanswered. Each rejection chipped away at her, making her feel worthless and foolish.

Her world was quieter without him in it, and the silence hurt. Her friends had tried to console her, telling her she'd get over it, that it was just a phase. But how could they understand? They hadn't been there during the late-night talks or the comfort they felt from being together. They hadn't felt the rush of being in love for the first time.

Lena found herself retreating into her room more often, scrolling through photos of their summer adventures, the images of them smiling together in the sunlight now haunting her. She felt like a fool for believing it would last, for thinking that

Copyright material from Angela Milliken-Tull (2025), *What Students Want From Their PSHE In Secondary School*, Routledge.

something so magical could survive the harshness of reality. Her heart felt heavy, and the ache was constant, like a dull throb she couldn't escape.

At school, she tried to keep it together. She wore a mask, pretending everything was fine, but every time Noah passed her in the hall, her chest tightened, and her mind spiralled with questions. Was he thinking about her at all? Had he ever felt the same way? Was she just some summer fling to him, nothing more than a fleeting distraction?

One afternoon, after weeks of avoiding it, Lena finally found herself standing outside the spot where she and Noah had first met. It had been their secret place, where they would talk and laugh and kiss, where she had felt safe and loved. Now, it felt empty, just another reminder of everything she had lost.

Tears welled up in her eyes, and she didn't care if anyone saw her. It was a strange and terrifying feeling, knowing that life would go on without Noah, and she would have to find a way to keep moving forward but, in that moment, she didn't know how to get over her heartache.

Discussion questions

1. What could have led to the relationship ending so suddenly?
2. Suggest some strategies Lena could use help manage her emotions when things feel overwhelming.
3. What could Lena do to help her move on from the breakup?

Scenario 2 - Give me respect! (suitable for age 11+)

JJ, a 14-year-old student, feels a constant pressure at school. Lately, he's struggled to manage his emotions, especially after a series of frustrating incidents including being accused of ruining his rugby team's chances of winning the county cup by dropping the ball, allowing the opposition to score a last-minute try.

His teachers don't notice when he's trying to participate in class, often ignoring him in favour of his louder classmates.

During lunch, his friends joke around, but they sometimes tease him in ways that feel hurtful. One friend, Jake, even mimics JJ's quiet voice, calling it 'weird', and laughs with the group. The others join in, and JJ can't shake the feeling that they don't take him seriously or even want to hang out with him.

Copyright material from Angela Milliken-Tull (2025), *What Students Want From Their PSHE In Secondary School*, Routledge.

His frustration builds up, but he isn't sure how to express it. When he's ignored or belittled, he tries to push through, but it always feels like no one understands. One day, JJ snaps after another round of being dismissed in class and mocked by his friends. During a group discussion, he lashes out at his classmates, snapping at Jake and saying things he doesn't mean, like calling him fake and saying he's not a real friend. In class, he throws a pencil across the room when a teacher dismisses his raised hand for the third time.

As the outbursts grow, JJ feels terrible, realising that his behaviour is becoming more problematic and worsening everything. He wonders if his frustration will ever be seen or respected and how he can manage his emotions without letting them control him.

Discussion questions

1. What do you think is causing JJ to feel so emotional?
2. Can JJ implement any strategies to help him manage his emotions better? Suggest some short-term things he can try as well as longer-term solutions.

Scenario 3 – I can't let you go (suitable for age 14+)

When Jason first met Emily, it felt like everything in his life had clicked into place. They'd spend hours texting, and laughing and could talk for hours. She made him feel special in a way no one else had. Their relationship was his anchor, the one thing in his life that made him feel like he mattered. But then, just 2 months after they started dating, Emily broke up with him.

Jason didn't understand. It wasn't supposed to end like this. They were perfect together, or so he thought. Emily said it was over because she needed space, but Jason couldn't accept that. Whenever he thought about her, his stomach twisted, his heart ached. He believed deep down that they were meant to be together. So, instead of moving on, he began obsessing over what went wrong.

At first, he would cycle or walk by her house late at night, watching the lights go out in her window. He'd hang around for hours, hoping to catch a glimpse of her walking out the front door, maybe even talking to her. When that didn't work, he started finding excuses to walk past her at school to see if she was with anyone else. He'd constantly follow her social media, replaying her old posts and pictures repeatedly, trying to find some sign that she still cared.

The idea of moving on seemed impossible. Jason told himself it was just because he loved her so much that he couldn't let go. He didn't realise how his obsession was starting to control him.

One day, he learned Emily was going to a party with friends. He hadn't been invited to the party and his jealousy flared. He couldn't bear the thought of her moving on with someone else. His mind spiralled, and he decided he had to see her that night, talk to her and make her see that they belonged together.

He showed up uninvited. He watched from a corner as Emily and her friends laughed, danced and enjoyed themselves. He felt a sense of anger rise within him. She didn't need to be with those people. She needed to be with him. But when she saw him lurking in the corner her face turned pale. She stepped away from her friends and told him to leave, her voice trembling.

'Jason, this is not okay. I don't want you here. Please, leave me alone', she said, her eyes filled with fear.

But Jason couldn't stop. 'I just want you back, Emily. We can make it work. We were happy.'

Her words fell on deaf ears. He pushed closer, desperate for a second chance, a moment where she'd see how much he cared.

He left, but over the following days and weeks he started following her, confronting her on the street and becoming angry when she tried to ignore him. One day he reached to grab her on the street. Emily panicked and stepped back onto a busy road. A car swerved, narrowly avoiding her, but screeched to a halt.

Emily was shaken but unharmed, but the accident had drawn attention. People rushed to her side, and Jason stood at a distance, heart pounding, the reality of what he had done sinking in.

The police arrived, and Emily's parents were called. Jason was told to leave. In the following days, Emily cut off all contact, blocked him on social media, and told friends to keep him away. Jason's classmates whispered about him, some expressing concern, others disgust. The weight of his actions crushed him, but nothing hurt more than knowing Emily would never look at him the same way again.

Copyright material from Angela Milliken-Tull (2025), *What Students Want From Their PSHE In Secondary School*, Routledge.

Jason spent the following months in a fog of regret. He couldn't escape the haunting realisation that his inability to let go had almost cost someone their life – and worse, it had cost him the last shred of Emily's trust. The love he had once felt now felt suffocating and toxic, and he was left alone to confront the aftermath of his obsession.

Discussion questions

1. What impact did Jason's behaviour have on Emily?
2. How could Jason have behaved differently?
3. Do you think Jason has learned a lesson from this, or is he likely to repeat this behaviour?

This is a darker scenario, and Jason's stalking behaviour is unacceptable and illegal. It is a form of abuse and could have resulted in tragedy. Although rare, there have been instances of teenage relationships ending in tragedy – most notably the case of Holly Newton, who lost her life when her jealous ex-boyfriend stabbed her in 2023.

Summary

- It is essential to understand the strength of teenage emotions
- Acknowledge emotions and try to use strategies to help manage feeling
- Look out for red flags that may indicate unhealthy or unsafe relationships
- Seek help and support if worried about a relationship

5 If you don't take this seriously, why should I?
The importance of role models

Teachers delivering high-quality PSHE recognise that it is an invaluable curriculum area for preparing students with the knowledge, skills and values for future life. It can also positively contribute to academic performance (Banjeree et al. 2013).

Many high-performing schools have excellent PSHE/PD programmes and take a whole-school approach to ensure this vital curriculum area is fully integrated across their settings. On the other hand, some schools face multiple challenges and struggle to build effective programmes, and the reasons for this are complex and multi-faceted.

Barriers to good quality PSHE

Staff confidence

As mentioned previously, it's not uncommon for teachers to have received very little or no PSHE input during training, even though most will be expected to deliver it. This causes many teachers to feel unprepared and unsure about teaching a subject that can be quite challenging. For students, this can lead to inconsistent teaching or no lessons at all, as teachers choose to cover topics they are more comfortable with instead.

Limited CPD

Very much linked to staff confidence, a further barrier can be a lack of CPD in PSHE. With limited time and numerous competing priorities, opportunities to increase teacher empowerment in PSHE via whole-school training can be challenging. There may not be anyone in school suitably experienced in delivering PSHE, or the PSHE lead may be in a relatively junior role and lacking confidence in providing whole-school CPD.

Lack of profile

Schools are judged on various outcomes, including personal development within which PSHE sits. However, despite the synergy between personal growth and academic achievement, exam results are almost always the critical benchmark by which schools are judged. In this respect, the core academic curriculum is viewed more favourably, and it is not unusual for time to be taken from PSHE for activities that are perceived as more important. However, schools with an ethos promoting social and emotional learning can see improvements in academic results (Banjeree et al., 2013; CASEL 2024).

Given the limited time allocated to PSHE by many schools, this conveys to students and staff that it is not an important subject. Where schools choose to share the timetabled allocation with another subject, for example, religious education, or try to squeeze PSHE sessions into short tutor sessions, they underscore the lowly position of PSHE.

Poor leadership

Teachers leading PSHE are almost always committed to developing and delivering high-quality sessions that meet the needs of students. However, this role is often given to staff at a relatively early stage in their career, so they may find themselves in a leadership role without widely recognised and accepted authority. This can make it challenging to monitor the quality and consistency of the programme, particularly where more senior colleagues are responsible for some of the delivery. This can be exacerbated if there is no backing from senior leadership.

When working with a group of teachers completing a leadership in PSHE qualification, several commented that the areas within their leadership journey that they found most challenging were negotiation, delegation and collaboration. With some colleagues experiencing the barriers mentioned above, their roles as PSHE leads were not always straightforward. However, all acknowledged the benefits it offered as they journeyed towards more senior leadership roles within education.

Resource limitations

Accessing good quality resources to help PSHE teaching is a further barrier to providing an effective programme. The material is unlikely to appeal to students if it is outdated or inflexible. Inadequate supporting notes for teachers will also make lessons less productive, and over-reliance on external providers is expensive and makes it more challenging to respond to student needs as they occur and evidence a well-embedded programme in the setting. Equally, the fast-changing pace of PSHE makes it difficult for teachers to keep on top of preparing lessons. The curriculum covers a wide range of topics, and it is unlikely that many teachers will have suitable expertise, underpinning the need for reliable, up-to-date material.

How to show your school takes PSHE seriously

Lead from the top

Like any other business, the messages about what an organisation stands for and its expectations from stakeholders come from the top. A senior leader with responsibility for PSHE, possibly within a wider pastoral remit, will demonstrate to staff that it's a critical curriculum area and should be given the same level of professionalism as any other subject. There are obvious links between safeguarding, mental health and PSHE and whole-school CPD led by the leads in these areas, effectively presenting a unified approach will demonstrate the school's commitment to this curriculum area.

Senior leadership role-modelling a positive and meaningful approach towards PSHE will help validate the subject. However, this should go together with acknowledging the difficulties staff may experience in teaching PSHE, implementing a regular CPD programme, and how it supports medium- and long-term plans.

Student consultation

Taking a regular temperature check of students' views about PSHE is essential. However, other questions will give insight into how well-embedded and beneficial the programme is. Over the past few years, teachers have been increasingly concerned about the increased prevalence of misogyny in school, often owing to greater awareness and support of individuals with a large online following. Asking students via a questionnaire about their views on misogyny and whether they have experienced it could be controversial and presents a somewhat narrow focus. A more helpful approach would be to consider the broader understanding of respect, for example, between peers and between students and staff.

Teacher influence

We also know that staff role modelling is very powerful in helping shape students' behaviour and values; this is a further area where insights can be useful. A school with well-embedded PSHE will probably be modelling respectful behaviour across all interactions within the setting.

As role models, teachers are highly influential and can provide life-changing support. This can be especially important for young people with fewer positive influences outside of school. As a teacher, you can almost certainly reflect on a former teacher who influenced your life and perhaps inspired you to become a teacher yourself. There will also be a few students you can instantly recall and with certainty will know that you were a positive influence on them, perhaps at a time when they were struggling or unsure about their next steps.

However, there will be others that you have influenced without even knowing it. As a young teacher, I unknowingly provided support for a student, and it was only when her mother shared in a parent's evening meeting that her daughter had decided to apply to university 'because of me' that I became aware of my role. The student in question was quiet in class, a little sullen and didn't participate much in discussion. Her work was ok but showed promise. I would regularly check in with her and give encouraging written feedback on assignments, and that was all it took. Noticing her without forcing participation while providing feedback was the right approach for her. Her mother also explained that she was divorced, which had been upsetting for her daughter, and as a police officer, she worked shifts, so she was not always as available as she would like.

Being a role model is often about noticing all your students and being seen as someone who cares about them. Sometimes quieter students get overlooked, particularly if they aren't emitting warm vibes. You won't always receive feedback that you've been a positive influence, but by being present, caring and viewing each student as an individual, you are being a positive role model.

Figure 5.1 shows a new question added to the 'How Are You?' student voice survey (Chameleon 2024). Responses from over 11,000 students aged 11–18 years (academic year 2023/2024) were received.

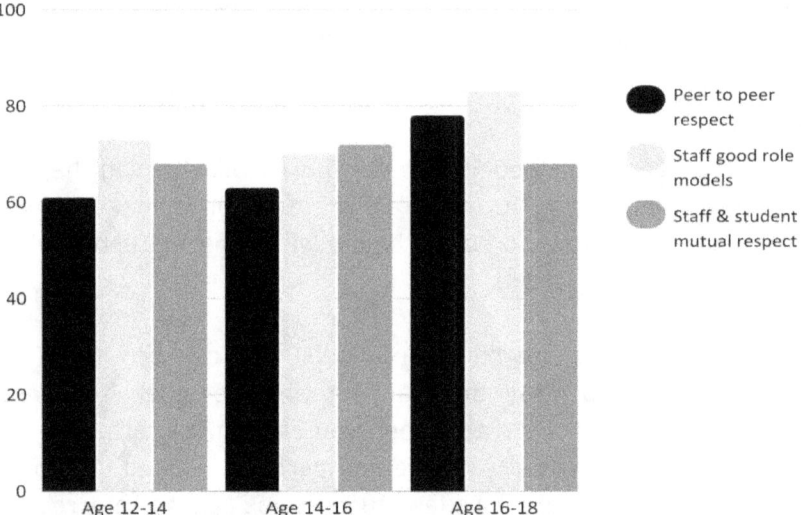

Figure 5.1 Views on peer-to-peer respect, staff as positive role models and staff-to-student respect

Peer-to-peer respect appears to increase as students get older, with an increase of nearly 20% in the number reporting that they 'strongly agreed or agreed' that peers respected each other.

Mutual respect between staff and students is consistent, with 68% in the younger age group strongly agreeing or agreeing with this statement, a modest increase to 72% in the age 14-16 group and then a slight fall back to 68%.

When asked about staff being good role models, there is a significant increase between the youngest and older groups, with 83% of post-16 students strongly agreeing or agreeing that this is the case.

Within settings, there were some variations. However, there tended to be a strong correlation between students reporting PSHE's usefulness and higher levels of respect and good staff role modelling reported. Chapter 7 picks up on the theme of staff role modelling and provides some tips for being a great role model.

Figure 5.2 compares student's reporting usefulness of PSHE across two academic years.

Settings regularly consulting with students via anonymous online surveys find a general upward trend in how PSHE is viewed. It is likely that those schools are actively working towards adaptive programmes that meet student needs, and this is reflected in more positive feedback.

Asking for student views, feeding back how those findings will be acted upon, and building this into a regular cycle demonstrates that teachers are taking PSHE seriously. It also exemplifies the plan, do, review approach that applies to other subject areas and many walks of life beyond education. All too often, surveys are completed and results are never shared with respondents. Skills frequently discussed and practised in PSHE sessions include many forms of communication, including presentations, active listening and negotiating. If teachers can role-model these skills and demonstrate the school's respect for co-creating a needs-based PSHE programme, it soon becomes a subject worth taking seriously.

% of students who think their PSHE is useful

2022/23

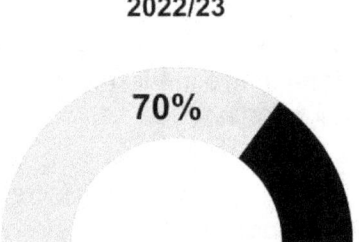

70% of age 12-14 students report that they find their PSHE 'sometimes', 'mostly', or always useful

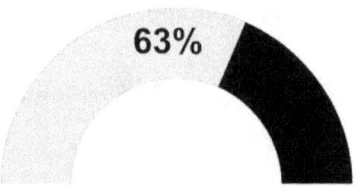

63% of age 14-16 students report that they find their PSHE 'sometimes', 'mostly', or always useful

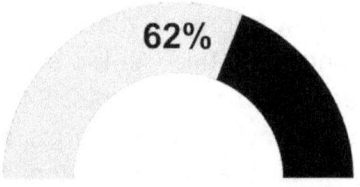

62% of age 16-18 students report that they find their PSHE 'sometimes', 'mostly', or always useful

2023/24

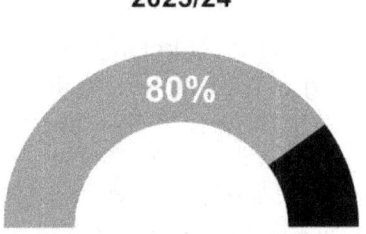

80% of age 12-14 students report that they find their PSHE 'sometimes', 'mostly', or always useful

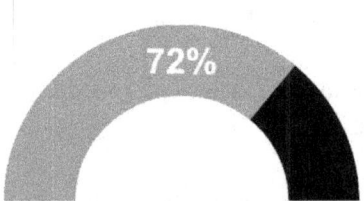

72% of age 14-16 students report that they find their PSHE 'sometimes', 'mostly', or always useful

68% of age 16-18 students report that they find their PSHE 'sometimes', 'mostly', or always useful

Figure 5.2 Usefulness of PSHE

CASE STUDY

Catherina Carragher, an Assistant Head Teacher at Garden International School in Malaysia

So, what things are schools doing that lead to very high levels of respect, reports of excellent staff role modelling, and students reporting significantly higher than average satisfaction with their PSHE programme? Does this impact academic results?

To help answer this question, Catherina Carragher discusses the PSHE and wellbeing programme.

The school has asked students to complete the 'How Are You?' survey for the past 3 years. The results are excellent, and the students report very high levels of respect for each other and staff. Almost all students 'agree' or 'strongly agree' that staff are good role models, and they are also very complimentary about the usefulness of their PSHE lessons. The school also enjoys excellent academic results.

At Garden International School (GIS), the tutor-time and PSHE programme have become a cornerstone of the school's culture and climate, and one of the primary vehicles for establishing effective relationships between students and teachers. The school's commitment to social and emotional learning is reflected in dedicated timetabled lessons, ensuring consistent delivery of this crucial aspect of student development.

The written curriculum and resources for PSHE are subject to the same rigour as other subject areas. Our Heads of Year are subject leads for PSHE and are supported by a senior leader to ensure consistency in standards throughout the school. The Heads of Year maintain a comprehensive curriculum document that provides teachers with clear guidance and students with a coherent learning journey. They have designated meeting time to discuss PSHE with their year team and provide professional development on topics where teachers might feel they lack expertise or confidence. They also monitor the quality of teaching and learning within PSHE through learning walks, using their observations to shine a light on good practice. The Heads of Year at GIS hold a considerable amount of authority and influence. This approach elevates the status of PSHE within the school community and ensures that it receives the resources and attention it deserves.

In addition to the professional development sessions held during year team meetings, there are regular whole-school opportunities for teacher development that certainly help support teaching and learning in the PSHE classroom. These have included whole-school staff briefings, and small group professional learning communities (PLCs) covering topics such as 'talking about controversial issues' and interculturalism in the classroom. From a pedagogical standpoint, we encourage teachers to take a dialogic approach in the PSHE classroom. By approaching class discussion with curiosity and resisting the urge to be the 'all-knowing' expert, teachers can create a more inclusive and interactive environment. This approach also ensures that teachers feel confident and equipped to handle sensitive topics, thereby modelling effective communication and critical thinking for students.

Inclusivity is also a key consideration when planning PSHE content. Teachers are directed by Heads of Year to adapt resources to ensure they reflect the diverse experiences of all pupils, taking into account language needs of English as an additional language learners and the requirements of students receiving learning support, as well as different cultures, values and beliefs. This approach helps students connect with the content and demonstrates respect for diversity. As a result, it fosters a strong sense of mutual respect between students and teachers at GIS. Our aim is to ensure that students see the relevance of PSHE to their daily lives and future aspirations, which our data suggest contributes to higher levels of engagement and satisfaction.

Student voice plays a crucial role in the success of the tutor time and PSHE programme at GIS. In addition to a yearly survey on pupil attitudes to self and school, we commission an anonymous survey specifically for PSHE to learn more about the behaviours and beliefs of our students. The results of this survey help shape the PSHE provision for the year and provide useful headline data, which are shared with students and parents. Students respond to a wellbeing questionnaire every 3 weeks, which helps facilitate meaningful one-to-one conversations between them and their tutors. We also conduct brief surveys after each extended PSHE session, providing immediate feedback on lesson effectiveness. This data is used to improve future sessions and identify and celebrate good teaching practices. The creation of a student panel to review PSHE provision further empowers students and ensures that the curriculum remains relevant to their needs.

KEY TAKEAWAYS

Acknowledge that PSHE is challenging for many teachers, and CPD is vital to build knowledge and confidence.

Accept that teachers are influential role models for their students, and that a positive and professional approach to PSHE will raise the subject's profile.

Aspire to provide a needs-based co-created PSHE curriculum based on stakeholder consultation.

PERSONAL REFLECTIONS

1. Is PSHE taken as seriously as it should be in your setting? Do students report satisfaction with their PSHE lessons?

2. Does the senior leadership team role ensure that PSHE and the wider personal development and wellbeing curriculum is fully embedded across the school?

3. What do you do to ensure you are a positive role model for your students?

FURTHER READING

Brookfield, Stephen D (2017) *Becoming a Critically Reflective Teacher*, Jossey-Bass

LESSON PACK

The resource to support this chapter is a CPD session on misogyny and sexual harassment.

There has been growing concern in schools about misogynistic online content and lack of respect towards girls and women. Greater awareness about violence towards women and girls means that we need to be equipped to provide students with knowledge and skills to act respectfully and the consequences of not doing so. At the same time, we must take an approach that does not alienate men and boys.

This CPD session will provide insight into this issue and the rationale behind the design of the accompanying teaching resources.

The lesson pack, Misogyny, causes and consequences, is the accompanying resource for Chapter 7.

RESOURCES

Auditing your PSHE provision

In recent years, there has been increasing concern about sexual harassment, misogyny and peer-on-peer abuse in schools. The murder of Sarah Everard in 2021, the reports to 'Everyone's Invited', which reached over 50,000, and increased awareness around violence towards women and girls have all contributed to this issue being part of the conversation in schools. In 2021, Ofsted and the Independent School's Inspectorate (ISI) completed a thematic review to answer the following questions:

- What is the scale and nature of sexual abuse in schools?
- How does the current safeguarding system listen to children's and young people's voices?
- To what extent do schools know about sexual abuse? When they do know, how do they respond?
- How well are multi-agency safeguarding arrangements working?

Various changes were implemented following the publication of the thematic review, and PSHE has a vital role in this area, causing as much concern as ever. The murder of schoolgirl Holly Newton was another tragic example of power imbalance resulting in tragedy.

Whether you are a class teacher, PSHE lead or in any other role in the school, the audit below can help you reflect on how your school is addressing sexual abuse, harassment and misogyny. There is also a link that will take you to an accredited CPD course.

This audit tool can be used to identify where specific aspects of your PSHE support statutory safeguarding obligations. This can provide evidence of curriculum coverage and progression and help you identify any gaps or duplication in provision. It is also useful evidence that can support questions that may arise during inspection visits.

Aspects of personal development are likely taught in subjects other than PSHE/Health and wellbeing, such as science, citizenship, computing, religious education, etc. When identifying gaps or duplication it is useful to liaise with relevant subject leads to assist with completing this audit.

The tool is organised into three age phases, allowing you to map out progression if desired. Some topics are only present in certain age groups owing to their age-appropriateness. Care should be taken with the timing of some concepts. You should aim for age-appropriate content to be introduced early and then built upon year on year in a spiral progression. Some topics can also trigger students (and staff), so be mindful of how an emotionally safe learning space is created.

Theme/concept	Subject(s) where this is taught	Year group(s)	Resources used	Actions, e.g. find replacement resource, update resource, bin resource, etc.
Ages 11–14				
Personal safety				
Gang culture				
Knife crime				
County lines				
Child criminal exploitation				
Trafficking				
Modern day slavery				
Radicalisation				
Personal safety				
Homelessness				
Drugs and alcohol				
Illegal substances				
Alcohol				
Tobacco/vaping				
Peer influence				
Initiations (e.g. dares to be in a group)				
Sex and relationships				
Forced marriage				
Honour-based abuse				
Female genital mutilation				
Consent				
Sexual harassment				
Misogyny				
Sexting				

Copyright material from Angela Milliken-Tull (2025), *What Students Want From Their PSHE In Secondary School*, Routledge.

Theme/concept	Subject(s) where this is taught	Year group(s)	Resources used	Actions, e.g. find replacement resource, update resource, bin resource, etc.
Upskirting				
Child sexual exploitation				
Grooming				
Sexual health				
Pornography				
Harassment (non-sexual)				
Stalking				
Bullying				
Online bullying				
Peer-on-peer abuse				
Coercion				
Emotional wellbeing				
Mental ill health				
Mental health strategies				
Emotional abuse				
Online abuse				
Self-harm*				
Disordered eating*				
Rights and responsibilities				
Equality Act (including the protected characteristics)				
Prejudice				
Discrimination				
LGBTQ+				
Ages 14-16				
Personal safety				
Gang culture				
Knife crime				
County lines				
Child criminal exploitation				

Theme/concept	Subject(s) where this is taught	Year group(s)	Resources used	Actions, e.g. find replacement resource, update resource, bin resource, etc.
Trafficking				
Modern day slavery				
Radicalisation				
Personal safety				
Physical assault				
Homelessness				
Drugs and alcohol				
Illegal substances				
Alcohol				
Tobacco/vaping				
Peer influence				
Initiations (e.g. dares to be in a group)				
Sex and relationships				
Domestic abuse				
Neglect				
Forced marriage				
Honour-based abuse				
Consent				
Sexual abuse				
Sexual harassment				
Misogyny				
Sexting				
Upskirting				
Rape/sexual assault				
Child sexual exploitation				
Grooming				
Sexual health				
Pornography				
Harassment (non-sexual)				
Stalking				

78 *What Students Want from their PSHE in Secondary School*

Theme/concept	Subject(s) where this is taught	Year group(s)	Resources used	Actions, e.g. find replacement resource, update resource, bin resource, etc.
Bullying				
Online bullying				
Peer-on-peer abuse				
Coercion				
Emotional wellbeing				
Mental ill health				
Mental health strategies				
Emotional abuse				
Online abuse				
Self-harm*				
Disordered eating*				
Suicide*				
Rights and responsibilities				
Equality Act (including the protected characteristics)				
Prejudice				
LGBTQ+				
Discrimination				
Ages 16-18				
Personal safety				
Gang culture				
Knife crime				
County lines				
Child criminal exploitation				
Trafficking				
Modern day slavery				
Radicalisation				
Personal safety				
Physical assault				
Homelessness				

Theme/concept	Subject(s) where this is taught	Year group(s)	Resources used	Actions, e.g. find replacement resource, update resource, bin resource, etc.
Drugs and alcohol				
Illegal substances				
Alcohol				
Tobacco/vaping				
Peer influence				
Initiations (e.g. dares to be in a group)				
Sex and relationships				
Domestic abuse				
Neglect				
Forced marriage				
Honour-based abuse				
Consent				
Sexual abuse				
Sexual harassment				
Misogyny				
Sexting				
Upskirting				
Rape/sexual assault				
Child sexual exploitation				
Grooming				
Sexual health				
Pornography				
Harassment (non-sexual)				
Stalking				
Bullying				
Online bullying				
Peer-on-peer abuse				
Coercion				

Copyright material from Angela Milliken-Tull (2025), *What Students Want From Their PSHE In Secondary School*, Routledge.

Theme/concept	Subject(s) where this is taught	Year group(s)	Resources used	Actions, e.g. find replacement resource, update resource, bin resource, etc.
Emotional wellbeing				
Mental ill health				
Mental health strategies				
Emotional abuse				
Online abuse				
Self-harm*				
Disordered eating*				
Suicide*				
Rights and responsibilities				
Equality Act (including the protected characteristics)				
Prejudice				
LGBTQ+				
Discrimination				

* It is important to avoid content that provides instruction on ways of self-harming, restricting food/inducing vomiting, hiding behaviour from others, etc., or that might provide inspiration for pupils who are more vulnerable (e.g. personal accounts of weight change or suicide attempts).

6   So, what has this got to do with me?
The importance of relevance in PSHE

PSHE is a broad curriculum designed to prepare students with the knowledge, skills and values that will help prepare them for navigating life at and beyond school. There is enormous variation in schools across the UK and beyond, and even schools within the same town or city can have quite different cohorts of young people attending.

Given the wide range of students and settings, it's fair to assume that the same PSHE content will not be equally relevant to all. However, we often experience knee-jerk reactions to PSHE content being delivered, owing to issues hitting the headlines.

> The world is fascinating, wonderful and terrifying. There's so much to learn and think about, but as a teenager, my world consisted of my friends and our day-to-day interactions!
>
> *Eleanor, journalism student, age 22*

Everyone vapes, don't they?

Over the past few years, vaping has evolved from being a smoking cessation tool aimed at adults trying to give up smoking cigarettes to a much more accessible 'trendy' option primarily owing to clever marketing targeted at young people.

There has been a significant increase in young people choosing to vape, and the press has run several stories sensationalising the rise in students vaping and the dangers associated with it. The language used when discussing young people's vaping habits leads us to believe that it has reached epidemic proportions, with *all* young people vaping and being unable to get through lessons without a toilet break to top up on their nicotine hit. The truth is that although there has been a rise in vaping, and this increases with age, most young people do not vape.

Figure 6.1 demonstrates this, and having data from your students is a good way of opening up discussions about what is relevant to your cohort. For example, you

DOI: 10.4324/9781032724638-6

82 What Students Want from their PSHE in Secondary School

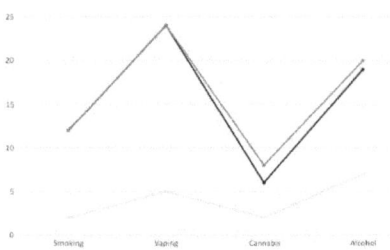
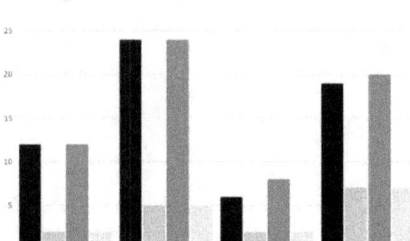
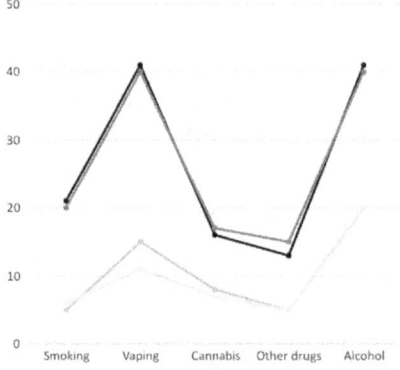
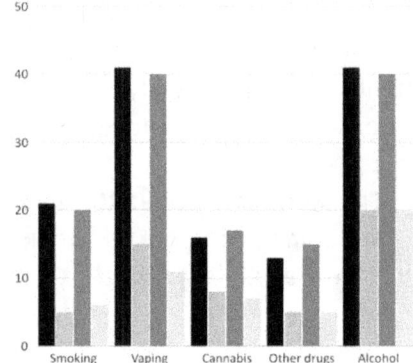
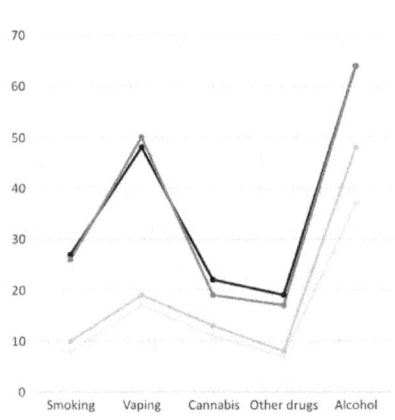
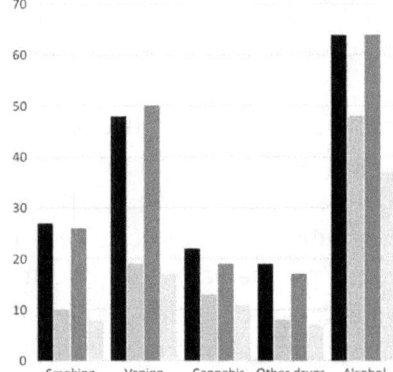

Figure 6.1 What the quotes could be referring to

should point out that although very few vape or smoke, there are high levels of misperception surrounding these behavioural choices. This can open discussions about media influence and how to be discerning about what is delivered by the media.

In this way, you can build on issues that may not be relevant to everyone, e.g. vaping, smoking, drug or alcohol use, to develop skills that are beneficial to everyone, namely, the ability to discern fact from fiction and to question and potentially dispel the myths surrounding many topics, particularly those associated with young people's behaviour.

British school children topping alcohol consumption charts

In April 2024, following the publication of the four-yearly report of the World Health Organisation (WHO) on school-age children's health behaviours, there were many headlines about the high level of alcohol consumption amongst British schoolchildren. The survey was conducted across 44 countries, and included 11-, 13- and 15-year-olds in England, Scotland and Wales, totalling around 4500 respondents. Findings showed that over a third of children had consumed alcohol by age 11. By the age of 13, 57% of girls and 50% of boys had drunk alcohol, and most 15-year-olds (67% of boys and 73% of girls) reported that they had access to alcohol.

The WHO study is interesting because it gives a broad overview of secondary school-age children's health-related behaviours across different locations. The dataset includes several European and Asian countries and also includes Canada. The study included smoking, vaping and other health indicators. However, understanding what is happening with your students in your school is more valuable than large, generalised datasets (World Health Organisation, 2024).

Alcohol is prevalent and widely accepted in most parts of British society. Young people's easy access to alcohol is a health concern, as early drinking increases the risk of alcohol-related harm, including dependency, in later years.

When surveying students about alcohol, it can be more helpful to ask how regularly they are drinking rather than for a simple yes or no response. Self-reporting on the quantity consumed or being drunk can also be misleading, as many people do not understand what a unit of alcohol is, and being drunk is often not accurately reported.

Using social norms and social marketing approaches to dispel myths about the frequency and quantity of alcohol consumption can also help reduce the incidence of drinking in students (Jones et al., 2017; Perkins, 2002).

The alcohol question related to the data presented in Figure 6.1 refers to the combined figure of students reporting that they regularly drink alcohol, defined as more than once per month. There is a large gap between the perception of drinking levels among peers and the actual level of drinking taking place. However, as students age, this gap narrows, as can be seen in Figure 6.1.

However, looking at results for individual schools, there will be instances where alcohol consumption is much lower than this figure, for example, where there is a large Muslim population. In this circumstance, the requirement for PSHE lessons about alcohol may be less relevant other than for students to understand the effects of alcohol on individuals that they may encounter and its impact on society.

There are few media headlines less harrowing than those confirming a young life lost as a result of violence involving a knife or other sharp object. An investigation by *The Independent* gathered data from 27 of the 43 police forces in England and Wales in April 2024 and reported on the incidences of knife attacks and reports of possession of a knife in schools (Ross, 2024). The highest incidence was in London. Across other areas, figures varied. However, numbers were small, often single figures. Despite the small numbers in proportion to the number of students and schools across the country, the potential consequences of possessing a knife or sharp implement are severe. The fallout for schools and the wider community when a knife attack takes place, although rare, can be devastating.

Once again, care should be taken when presenting data from national or regional reports, as they may not represent your setting, and students may view the figures as lacking relevance.

When gathering data about carrying knives or sharp implements, it's vital to be able to filter out references to small craft knives, scissors or a compass. In my data collection, the follow-up question requests that students report why they carry a knife, with one option being 'for personal protection'. This response is a red flag, as research from the Youth Endowment Fund shows that carrying a knife puts individuals at a higher risk of being harmed (Popham, 2024).

It is useful to gain insight into how many students in your setting are carrying a knife. However, some results are not appropriate to share with students, and this is one of them. The exception is if there were no reports of carrying a knife or sharp implement for 'own protection'.

Figure 6.2 shows perception vs. reality data about carrying a knife by age group. The percentages are low, and although there is still a gap between students who

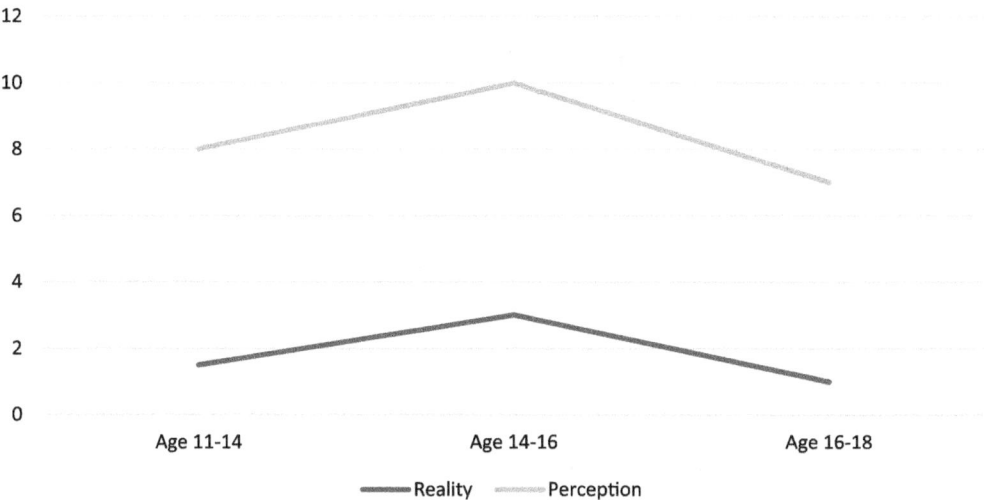

Figure 6.2 Percentage reality vs. perception: carrying a knife by age group

do not realise just how low the incidence of knife-carrying is, they do not perceive prevalence to be very high.

Nonetheless, in this area, we aspire to zero results (Chameleon, 2024). Over 11,000 responses were collected from a varied range of school settings. In almost every setting at least one or two students reported carrying a knife.

With most other topics, we could give a very light touch in PSHE lessons if the incidence were very low. However, education on the dangers of knives is essential for all students, as just one knife in school could result in tragedy. Rural areas have experienced knife attacks, and although there is an increased risk in more highly populated areas, there is access to knives everywhere and, therefore, potential risk.

We often associate carrying a knife with boys and men, and girls may feel that this makes the topic less relevant to them. Interestingly, some girls do report carrying a knife, although far fewer do than boys. Girls have been victims of knife attacks, and when looking at healthy relationships and women's safety, which is relevant to everyone, there should be inclusion of femicide, which very often involves a bladed weapon.

Relevance by gender

There are remarkably few topics that are only relevant to one gender, even when considering women's health or, for that matter, men's health; most will have partners of the opposite sex, and single-sex partnerships are also likely to have close friends and family of the opposite sex. Understanding and empathising with the opposite gender is valuable learning for all young people. It will help them navigate all kinds of relationships, including intimate partnerships, as they mature and move towards adulthood.

A few areas stand out in terms of significant behavioural differences between girls and boys, and these will not come as a surprise. The data in Figures 6.3-6.6 filters by male or female gender only. Students selecting 'other' or 'prefer not to say' are not included as a separate category as the numbers are too small to analyse with any degree of accuracy (Chameleon, 2024).

Gambling

Boys are more likely to report that they have gambled compared with girls (Chameleon, 2024). Gambling is another topic that regularly hits the headlines, mainly related to a tragic event or a sporting scandal. When considering PSHE content around gambling to ensure that it is relevant to all students, gambling behaviour and potential addiction may resonate more with boys. However, the impact of gambling when out of control has a ripple effect that can be negative and touch the lives of friends and family, have health consequences and affect work and, of course, finances.

Younger people often turn to friends as a first line of support if worried about anything, so having the knowledge and skills to help a friend and being aware and confident to seek additional support where necessary is relevant to everyone. Whereas over 90% report that there is at least one friend they can turn to for

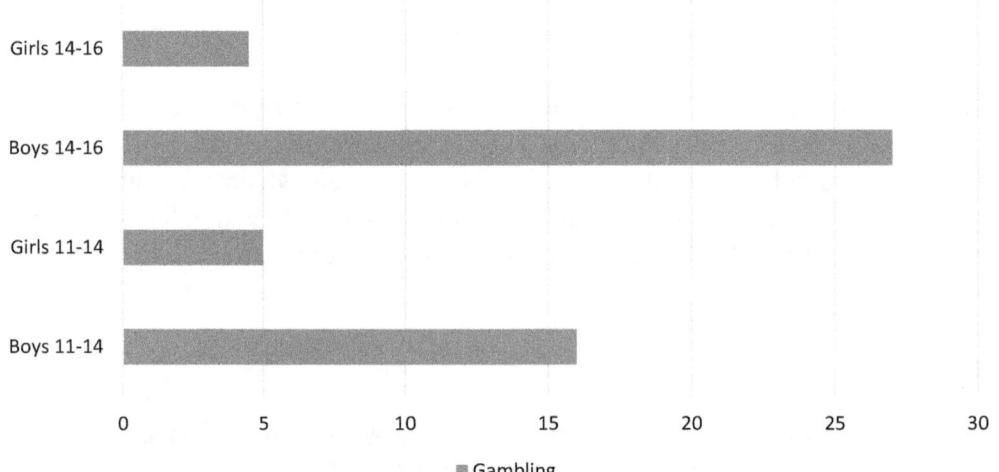

Figure 6.3 Percentage of students gambling (by gender)

support when it comes to identifying a staff member in school, the numbers drop off and can vary quite significantly across settings. Where students report good quality PSHE, this tends to correlate with higher numbers reporting that there are staff members they would ask for support if necessary.

Pornography

A common concern we regularly hear from various experts is that young people are learning about sex via pornography. An often-cited statistic is that by the age of 11, most children will have viewed pornography. As mentioned previously, care should be taken when interpreting the data presented as attention-grabbing headlines. The prevalence of smartphones, tablets and computers, together with children having access to their own devices, means it is much easier for children to encounter inappropriate content, including pornography. However, this does not mean that they are actively seeking porn. Algorithms can push a wide range of content to users when seemingly innocent search terms are used.

Chameleon (2024) survey data asks students if they *choose* to view pornography as opposed to coming across it accidentally. Results demonstrate that in younger students choosing to view porn is rare; however, as they get older, there is an increase. When results are filtered by gender, a significant difference exists between girls and boys. Therefore, in response to the statement that most young people get their sex education from pornography, this may be the case for some boys, but it is much less likely to be a relevant source for girls.

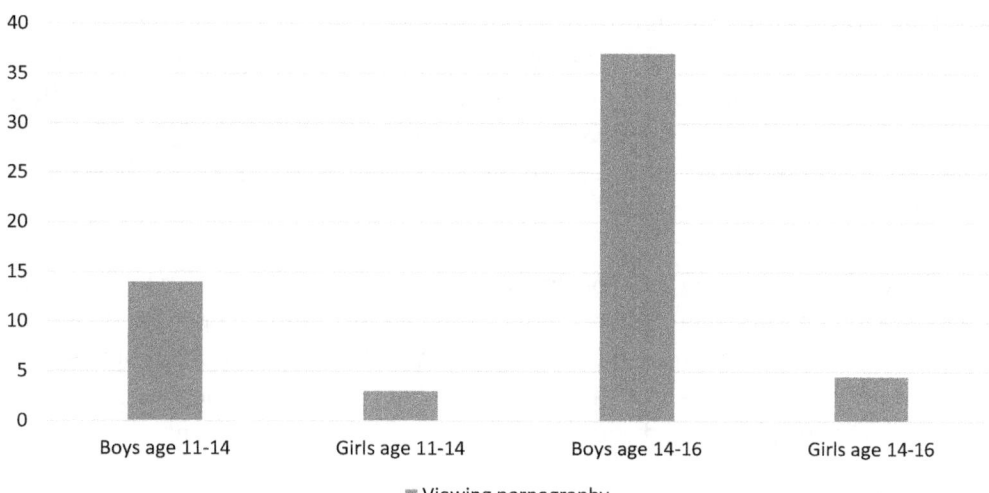

Figure 6.4 Students choosing to view pornography, boys vs. girls

In terms of the topics that students want more focus on in PSHE, pornography is in the top five but behind finance and first aid, and this is the case for both girls and boys. It is also a topic that staff can feel very uncomfortable about teaching, which is understandable. It is often an area where external providers will be invited to the school to deliver sessions, which can be impactful. However, this should always be designed to enhance a well-structured PSHE programme in school rather than replace it.

Once again, having data about your student's knowledge, behaviour and perceptions will allow you to tailor your programme to their needs.

Emotional and mental health

At a universal level, there are some questions we can ask that indicate how well students are managing their emotional and mental health. Adolescence is an emotionally charged time, and mental health is another area that regularly hits the headlines. A robust PSHE programme will address emotional and mental health, providing knowledge input and strategies to help students understand and manage their emotions. The aim is that a more 'upstream' approach, i.e. addressing some of the more uncomplicated day-to-day emotional ups and downs, will result in most students understanding and managing emotions better, leaving more time available for counsellors or other professionals in school to support students with more complex needs.

Data shows that girls report less positively on emotional health indicators (Chameleon 2024, Figure 6.5). They also request more input in PSHE lessons about mental health conditions and how to manage mental and emotional health. The reasons behind this difference between genders are likely to be multifaceted. They may include girls being more aware of emotional issues and therefore reporting them, students being at different stages of emotional maturity, more pressure on girls about physical appearance and the impact of fluctuating hormones.

The ongoing fallout from lack of socialisation during the COVID pandemic and subsequent lockdowns could also continue to manifest in young people in general and girls, in particular, experiencing difficulties with emotional or mental health. Undoubtedly, ongoing research in this area will help us better understand the long-term impacts on children and young people's emotional development.

So, what has this got to do with me? 89

I am happy/ok with my looks

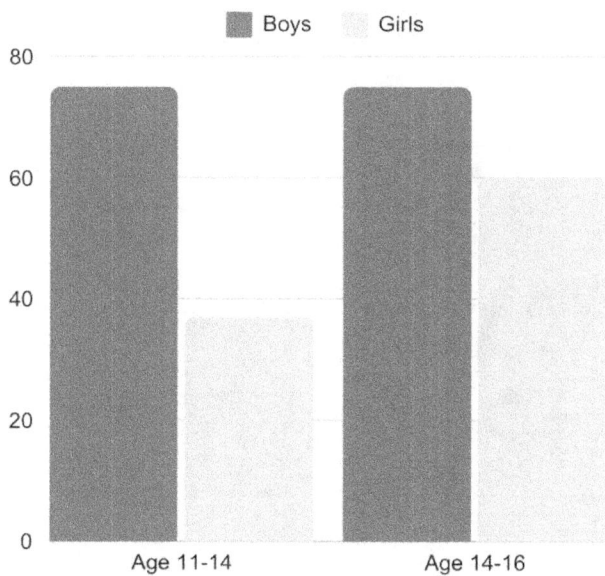

I try not to compare myself to others

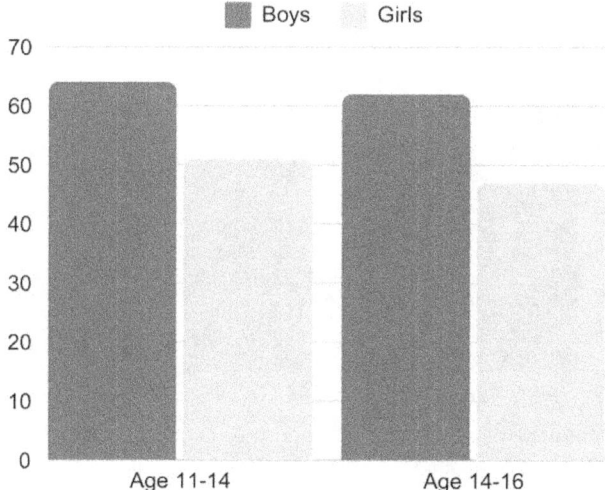

Figure 6.5 The percentage of students responding to proxy indicators of emotional/mental health, by gender

I have healthy ways to manage difficult emotions

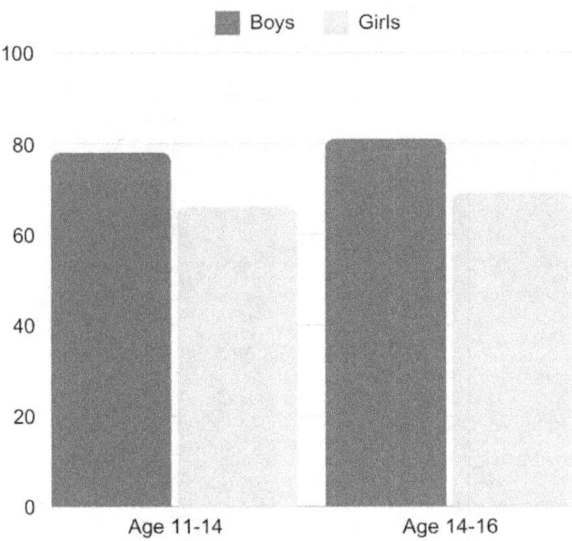

I can move forward from difficulties (resilience)

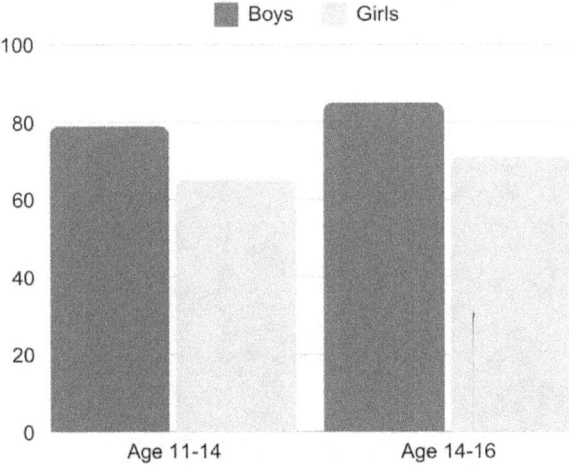

Figure 6.6 The percentage of students responding to proxy indicators of emotional/mental health, by gender

Suicide

Despite boys reporting more positively on emotional and mental health indicators, it would be overly simplistic to assume that this means they are mentally healthier. The latest data from the Samaritans show that suicide remains higher in men. There are regional variations, with London having the lowest rate of suicide. The Samaritans also report that numbers are very similar to pre-pandemic levels, concluding that there is no evidence that the number of suicides has increased as a result of the COVID-19 pandemic. (Samaritans, 2024).

Delivering lessons about suicide

It can be challenging to deliver lessons about suicide. However, this topic is very relevant, and most young people will have experienced the feelings associated with this loss, even if it is at a distance, for example, in the case of a high-profile celebrity.

- Lessons can take many directions but must be well-structured and set ground rules to ensure a safe learning environment.
- Awareness of the personal circumstances of students is also essential to allow any student who has experienced suicide in their family or friendship group to decide if they wish to take part in the lesson or not. This should also be the case for staff.
- There are charities providing resources and sessions in school that can be a valuable addition to your programme.
- Relevant mental health input and social and emotional learning should be a fundamental foundation of your PSHE and personal development programme.

What's relevant for twenty-first-century life?

Preparing students for an unknown future is an enormous challenge for schools. Some subject areas change more slowly, certainly at the level covered in school. However, as the use of AI increases to support research, the knowledge base across many topics changes more quickly.

On the other hand, a lot of PSHE content changes rapidly. Issues that concern young people or impact them emerge quickly, meaning that teachers need to be ready to adapt and change their lessons not only to meet the needs of students but also to adapt to the fast-paced change in what students are exposed to, and this can be on a global level.

Feedback from students sometimes includes comments about climate change or upsetting news stories; however, it's often parents who worry more about how these issues affect their children. Many teenagers are more concerned about the things that affect them on a fundamental day-to-day level. Their various relationships, including with themselves, fitting in, discovering who they are and being part of a tribe.

The more significant issues may seem far less relevant to many students; however, with maturity often comes a widening of the lens through which they see the world. As teachers, you cannot teach students about things that don't yet exist. However, you can make them aware of and provide opportunities to practise the skills identified as critical for the next generation of workers. PSHE sessions are a perfect forum for this and should dovetail with career lessons. There is more on this in Chapter 3.

CASE STUDY

In this case study Dr Bryony Jones discusses making PSHE relevant in a single-sex environment and the changes she has noticed in recent years about what students want in their PSHE lessons, as well as the challenges of fitting everything into limited time.

Dr Bryony Jones – Head of Department, Stratford Girls' School

I've been Head of Department for PSHE in a single-sex girls' grammar school for 8 years, and in that time the subject has changed enormously, especially in the amount of content that is now a statutory requirement. In truth, it's getting more and more difficult to fit the requirements into the time allowed for the subject, especially to cover them in a meaningful way, and I know we have a more generous time allowance than many schools. I always ask students what they would like to cover, and they are happy to share their thoughts, but I have to keep in mind that much of the timetabled lesson time needs to be given over to topics that are statutory. Fortunately, many of the topics students say they want to cover are ones that are required by law, which is just as well!

Our students take PSHE seriously and we are fortunate to have a teaching model that means that they largely have a consistent staff team. Staff who understand the topics, know what has been discussed in previous years and are confident to talk about SRE and Emotional and Mental Health, is vital in creating the understanding of 'what PSHE means in this school'.

Probably the single biggest and most evident change that I've seen over the years of teaching PSHE is students' attitudes towards talking about mental health. When we first introduced it as a topic years ago, a number of students in KS3 asked to be excused from lessons because they didn't feel able to talk about it. Now that never happens; students are very ready to have these conversations and are largely very

So, what has this got to do with me? 93

well informed about the topic. However, discussions tend to show that, although students *know* a lot of about how to keep themselves mentally healthy – just as much these days as they know about how to keep themselves physically healthy – they tend (and will readily admit to this) to *do* rather fewer of these things than they know they should. There is still a way to go, I think, for us as a society.

In terms of delivery styles, our students almost universally say they dislike role plays of any kind, even the students for whom drama is their thing, and this is especially true once they reach Year 9 and above. Across all Key Stages they appreciate having a variety of tasks within a lesson; they do like to write down some key facts about something at some point (and given the chance would prefer to write it down word-for-word from a PowerPoint slide to avoid getting it wrong) and they like to do short quizzes, but they don't want to spend a lot of lesson time writing. Their preference would be to work on projects where they have some autonomy, but that would often mean spending longer on a particular topic than curriculum time permits. Research tasks and presenting back about things they have learned are things they largely enjoy, although the reality of time constraints means that we often have less time than we would need to do these kinds of activities properly.

The majority of our lesson time is spent in discussions. Our students enjoy different types of discussions, but many prefer to talk about things with a partner, or as part of a small group of three or four students before offering contributions to whole-class discussions. We work hard to encourage participation, and to build up the confidence to participate, across as many students as possible, while keeping in mind that PSHE topics can be sensitive and an opt-out is important. Our students' fears – and the reasons why some are reluctant to contribute to whole-class discussions – are primarily of getting things 'wrong' or looking or feeling silly in front of other members of the class, and they also worry about offending others. Distancing techniques are our saviour, and we talk directly to students about the fact that it's often much easier to talk about how *someone* might feel in a particular situation than how *they themselves* feel. There's a certain vulnerability to disclosing something personal about your own fears, while this isn't the case if you're just trying to imagine how people might feel. Once students realise this, it really helps their conversations move forwards, especially if they're sitting next to someone they don't know particularly well yet.

Students also want to talk about gender and sexuality. They are interested, have opinions and want to know more. They really do want to understand different perspectives and they appreciate that things that may not be directly relevant to them personally may well be relevant to friends or members of their family. They want to, and can, talk about these issues with maturity and understanding. With SRE, our students want factual information delivered in a common-sense way, and I suspect that the single-sex nature of our setting makes these discussions more straightforward and sensible. There are sometimes comments from our students, especially when discussing relationships, that 'boys should be having these discussions too', which reveals a perception that they think they're not. I can only hope that their perception isn't correct, and that boys are having these same discussions, but it's an interesting point.

KEY TAKEAWAYS

Acknowledge that students may view some parts of the PSHE curriculum as irrelevant.

Accept that you will only sometimes be able to provide a programme that is 100% relevant to all students.

Aspire to have an evidence base identifying what is most relevant to your students and helping them understand the connections between topics and the underlying skills that will be relevant for their future lives and careers.

PERSONAL REFLECTIONS

1. Do you currently take steps to ensure your programme is relevant for your students? Is this a regular process? How is it carried out? Is your programme adapted accordingly?

2. Do PSHE, careers and mental health leads work collaboratively?

3. Do topics within your PSHE programme effectively connect broader personal development and the academic curriculum?

FURTHER READING

Youth Endowment Fund (2023) Children, Violence and Vulnerability, chrome-extension://efaidnbmnnnibpcajpcglclefindmkaj/https://youthendowmentfund.org.uk/wp-content/uploads/2023/11/YEF_Children_violence_and_vulnerability_2023_FINAL.pdf

World Health Organisation (2024) Health Behaviour in School Age-aged Children, https://www.who.int/europe/initiatives/health-behaviour-in-school-aged-children-(hbsc)-study

Organisations that support schools to teach about suicide

Papyrus, https://www.papyrus-uk.org/schools-guide/

Samaritans, https://www.samaritans.org/

LESSON PACK

Financial exploitation and 'sextortion'

This resource is a good example of the connection between and across topics in PSHE. This pack challenges students to consider a range of different types of financial exploitation, including 'sextortion', which may demand additional indecent images or money. There are links to coercion, mental health and online safety, as well as more traditional scams associated with financial exploitation. There are over 2 hours of activities and lots of opportunities for discussion and gauging understanding and progress.

FURTHER READING

Youth Endowment Fund (2024) Children, violence & vulnerability, https://youthendowmentfund.org.uk/news/70-of-teens-see-real-life-violence-on-social-media-reveals-new-research/#:~:text=The%20Youth%20Endowment%20Fund%20(YEF,online%20in%20the%20past%20year.

RESOURCES

Relevance

The activities to support this chapter aim to place young people at the centre of wider issues that may impact on their emotional and mental health.

There has been increasing concern about the apparent rise in mental health problems in children and young people. Given the turbulence of the teenage years, it is not surprising that mental health can suffer, and very often, this is short term and resolves with support from friends, family and school. Many young people can take a few simple steps to improve their mental health quickly, but for others, longer-term strategies and professional support will be required, which can be difficult to access.

The activities in this section aim to identify and understand some of the issues that can cause worry or concern to young people. It is not intended to be therapeutic and if you have specific concerns about any of your students don't hesitate to get in touch with your safeguarding lead.

Please use ground rules before commencing any PSHE session and return to them as often as is required during the lesson to ensure that students feel safe while working on potentially sensitive topics.

This activity can be used with students in secondary school. The material can be modified or extended depending on the maturity of the group you are working with.

Activity 1 - What causes anxiety?

Introduce the session by sharing the captions in Figure 6.7 that are quotes from young people describing things that make them feel anxious. Working in pairs or small groups, students discuss the captions and note what they believe is being referred to (Table 6.1). Give some time for discussion and then take some feedback. Students may have different suggestions about the quotes, which are equally valid.

Activity 2

The next stage in the activity is to give each group one or two of the statements to look at in more detail and challenge them to come up with some advice to give the young person to help them manage their feelings.

Give a few minutes for discussion, and then ask the groups to share their advice. Table 6.2 provides some ideas and suggestions.

Copyright material from Angela Milliken-Tull (2025), *What Students Want From Their PSHE In Secondary School*, Routledge.

So, what has this got to do with me? 97

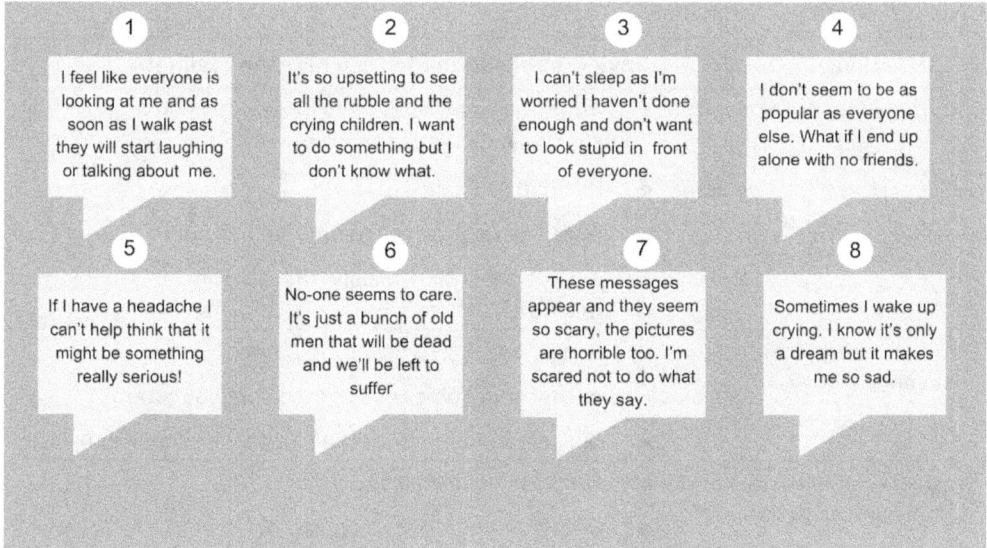

Figure 6.7 What the quote refers to

Table 6.1 What the quotes could be referring to

	What the quote might be about
1	Feeling nervous about how peers view them. This is a common feeling and can become problematic. If social situations become increasingly concerning some individuals can develop social anxiety. However, for most it is simply a lack of confidence and overthinking the situation.
2	World events can be worrying and upsetting. News coverage, particularly when graphic or featuring children can be difficult to watch. A sense of hopelessness can accompany this as the situation is beyond the control of the person watching it.
3	This may be worry about schoolwork or exams. It is natural to feel concerned about not doing well and also about how others may perceive them.
4	It is not unusual for individuals and particularly teenagers to compare themselves with others and usually this is not favourably. This can lead to a lack of self-confidence, which can make things worse and start a downward spiral.
5	Being able to go online to check symptoms means that some individuals discover a whole range of potential illnesses, many of which are extremely rare, that they self-diagnose with. Health anxiety can be debilitating and require professional support.
6	This quote may be about environmental issues which can be concerning for everyone but especially for young people who will face the consequences of inaction. This can also result in feelings of hopelessness.
7	It is likely that this quote is about something frightening online, either a message or picture that is frightening. This type of communication often plays on superstition and for individuals who are already anxious it can be very upsetting.
8	It is quite common for dreams to feel very real, and this includes dreams about loss, such as the death of a loved one.

Copyright material from Angela Milliken-Tull (2025), *What Students Want From Their PSHE In Secondary School*, Routledge.

Table 6.2 Strategies for managing feelings

	Situation	Advice/suggestions to help manage feelings
1	Judged by peers	• Aim to appear confident, head up, smile as they walk past, acknowledge the group • Positive self-talk • Hang around with a friend or in a group • Accept that it's unlikely that anyone is laughing or talking about you
2	Frightening world events	• Limit exposure to upsetting content • Accept that some things are out of your control • Support a charity that is helping in the conflict or disaster
3	Overwhelmed by schoolwork or exams	• Take control of the situation • List what you need to do and make a plan to achieve it • Don't leave things to the last minute • Positive self-talk – no-one is likely to be interested in your results or judge you on them
4	Unfair comparison	• Avoid over-exposure to social media that leads to self-criticism • Try to live in the moment, enjoy friendships and don't focus on what may or may not happen in the future • Positive self-talk • List the things that you like about yourself, and others compliment you on
5	Worried about health	• Try to avoid using 'Dr Google' • If worried about a health issue make an appointment with a GP • Acknowledge that most young people are healthy • Take control of your health by exercising, eating a varied diet, getting enough sleep. Spending time with friends, family, pets
6	Environmental concerns	• Limit exposure to information that will trigger anxiety about environmental issues • Accept that much of this is beyond our control • Do things that are within our control such as recycling, avoiding fast-fashion, reducing carbon footprint, reducing meat consumption • Support environmental groups

(Continued)

Table 6.2 (Continued)

	Situation	Advice/suggestions to help manage feelings
7	Online negative messaging	• Delete messages or images that are frightening or upsetting • Block the sender • Do not forward 'chain-letter' type messages • Report inappropriate content
8	Upsetting dreams	• Acknowledge that we do not understand the inner workings of the mind, including dreams • An emotional response to something upsetting is natural, accept it • Talk to someone you trust about the dream; they are likely to reassure you and may have experienced something similar • Be rational, chances are you have had a dream where you could fly or had a super-power and have acknowledged that this is not realistic either

Ask the group if there are any general themes emerging when considering the issues that can cause worry or concern?

1. Distinguish what can and cannot be controlled
2. Acknowledge the importance of perspective and positive self-talk
3. Limit exposure to information or situations that can be triggering

Extension activity

Research by the Youth Endowment Fund (2024) discusses growing anxiety amongst young people about spending time outside owing to exposure to frightening online content showing knives, other weapons and assaults. The online material often portrays exaggerated imagery and statistics, leading young people to believe that spending time outside meeting friends and making those all-important connections that are a vital part of socialisation are too dangerous to contemplate.

We know that the UK is a relatively safe society, most people do not carry weapons and murder and serious assaults are rare. What can be done to promote more balanced and truthful messages to children and young people?

Activity 3 – Avoiding the echo chamber

The way in which we receive information plays a significant role on how we then think about and share the issues we are interested in. Having some insight about this exposure can help us take a step back from the vast swathes of data we are bombarded with and be more discerning and considered about the information we receive and what we do with it.

Step back in time

Working individually, ask students to reflect on the questions in Figure 6.8, making a note of their answers.

After a few minutes, students can discuss their primary school experiences in pairs or small groups.

Ask the class to feedback what was different about their interests and communication compared with now:

- There was likely more time spent communicating face-to-face and much less information to sift through.
- More access to online content and mobile phones is needed now.
- There was more time spent in organised activities
- Exposure to the views and influence of unknown individuals was limited.

Think back to when you were at primary school...

- What were you interested in? (hobbies)
- Who were your friends?
- What did you spend you time doing?
- How did you communicate?
- Were you in any clubs or sports teams together?

Figure 6.8 My younger self

Copyright material from Angela Milliken-Tull (2025), *What Students Want From Their PSHE In Secondary School*, Routledge.

So, what has this got to do with me? 101

Share the information in Figure 6.9 and ask students to respond to the questions, highlighting any changes from when they were younger at primary school.

Take some feedback and ask students if they sometimes receive messages or advertising about something they have been talking about or reading online with friends. Can they suggest how this happens? Are they being spied on by mobile phones?

Take some feedback and discuss how algorithms promote messaging to young people or anyone else using search engines and social media (see Figure 6.10).

Working in small groups challenge students to write a short explanation about what the social media 'echo chamber' is. Aim to include an example of something they have experienced.

Some sentence starters could be:

- Every time we use social media algorithms . . .
- This can be useful . . .
- However, it can also cause the following problems . . .
- An example of this is . . .
- The echo chamber effect can feed into conspiracy theories by . . .
- A way to avoid being trapped in an echo chamber is to . . .

Compare this to now...

- What are your interests? (hobbies)
- Do you have online friends?
- How much time do you spend meeting friends face-to-face compared to online?
- How do you communicate?
- Do you find yourself communicating with people with similar views and interests?

Figure 6.9 My current self

Copyright material from Angela Milliken-Tull (2025), *What Students Want From Their PSHE In Secondary School*, Routledge.

> **A is for Algorithm**
>
> - Algorithms are sophisticated sets of rules and processes digital platforms use to determine which content is most relevant to users.
>
> - They analyse vast amounts of data, including user interactions, preferences, and behaviours, to create a personalised experience.
>
> - By examining search history, likes, shares, and time spent on content, algorithms can push content that aligns with a user's interests and habits.
>
> - The aim is to keep users engaged and on the platform for extended periods.
>
> - However, this can also lead to echo chambers, where users are predominantly exposed to content that reinforces existing beliefs, potentially limiting exposure to diverse perspectives.
>
> - As algorithms continue to evolve, balancing personalisation with diversity and accuracy remains a key challenge for technology companies.

Figure 6.10 Understanding algorithms

Give the group some time to discuss and prepare their explanations and then ask each group to share their explanation.

You may also have your own example to share.

7 Spare me the lecture!
Effective pedagogy in PSHE

Cast your mind back to university and remind yourself of that module that you really didn't enjoy. Chances are it was a passive learning situation where you attended a series of long lectures, at least an hour but possibly 2 hours, with a break in the middle. As a young adult with good reason to be there, i.e. complete your degree course, you probably had some in-built motivation that kept you turning up week after week, but no doubt the experience was unpleasant, maybe even painful.

For me, the number one spot for the most boring lecture ever goes to Macroeconomic Theory. It was a 2 hour lecture held in a large lecture theatre. The undoubtedly academically brilliant professor spoke in a hushed, high-pitched voice with a strong accent. The content was dense and complex, and we were encouraged to write copious notes and copy algebraic equations throughout. I can't remember anything about Macroeconomic Theory, but I do recall how utterly tedious it was; I feel the groan form at the mere thought of this experience and also the embarrassment when some students, mostly male, would interrupt to ask questions with double meanings that the lecturer didn't understand. Despite hating every moment of the session, most students did not want to see the lecturer disrespected.

This also happened in the 'olden days' when YouTube didn't exist, so there was no engaging expert to tune into with a cheerful explanation of what on earth macroeconomics was all about. Instead, it relied on academic textbooks, and I still have no idea how I passed the module.

Students do not enjoy a 'lecture-style' lesson even when they have signed up for it. While a few highly engaging individuals can enthral and hold our attention in a TED Talk, these tend to be relatively short, well-rehearsed and designed to entertain.

Concentration span

There is little to be gained from this approach as a teaching method. There is a lot of research on the attention span of adolescents, and according to experts, there

DOI: 10.4324/9781032724638-7

is a wide range of variability. Some experts suggest an upper concentration level of 40 minutes, while others believe that 10-20 minutes is more realistic – certainly not enough time to deliver a lecture.

Many factors will impact the ability to concentrate, including physical conditions such as hunger or fatigue, and the quality of the classroom environment. Are there many distractions? Is the temperature comfortable? Interest level, the difficulty of the task, how the content is delivered, and adolescent brain development will all play a role in concentration.

Pedagogy for PSHE

During your training and subsequent teaching career, you will have discovered many learning theories that you can employ to encourage secure attention, develop memory and knowledge, introduce and build challenges, and increase cognitive engagement.

Many of the strategies you use in your core teaching will be transferrable to PSHE. However, there are a few that you should avoid.

The importance of ground rules

A key aim of PSHE lessons is developing knowledge and skills within a safe and secure environment. This is true of all classes, but as PSHE explores potentially sensitive and controversial areas, there is a higher level of risk than in some other subjects. Ground rules are imperative, and these should be introduced at the start of every lesson and returned as frequently as required.

Ideally, students will co-create the ground rules, giving them greater ownership of the process and the agreed contract. You can task students with designing their ground rules using some starter questions:

- Why is it important to have agreed rules of behaviour in PSHE lessons?
- What will make this a safe learning environment for everyone?
- What should be included in our ground rules?

It is important to phrase the agreed ground rules positively, e.g. 'We will listen to each other' instead of 'We will not interrupt'. You may wish to couch the ground rules in terms of the 'rights' of each student in the class, as Figure 7.1 demonstrates. There may be an ethos in your school that can be reflected in the ground rules. The important thing is that they are owned by your students and used to support effective learning.

Confidentiality is likely to arise, and it is helpful to be transparent about safeguarding responsibilities, i.e. there are some circumstances, your responsibility as a teacher requires you to share information, even when it is given to you in confidence.

Figure 7.1 is an example of ground rules you could use as a basis for developing your own.

Active learning

We looked at examples of active learning in Chapter 3 and you will know what works well with your students and be able to consider what may be a good match within PSHE lessons. We've agreed that the 'sage on the stage' lecture is not appropriate but are there any other popular teaching strategies that may not effectively translate to PSHE lessons?

'No opt out'

Teach Like a Champion (Lemov, 2021) is a popular short read that many will be familiar with. Lemov encourages teachers to use a 'No opt-out' technique to embed consistent engagement and accountability. This involves asking a student for an answer; if they do not know it, another student provides the answer. The teacher returns to the original student and asks them to repeat the correct response. The aim is to reinforce the understanding that every student must engage in the learning process.

Would this be effective in PSHE? Could it be modified?

There is a conflict if the agreed ground rules include the right to pass. In PSHE including the right to pass in ground rules is recommended.

> **Rules of Engagement**
> - I have the right to share my opinion and be listened to
> - I have the right to pass
> - I have the right to be respected and valued
> - I have the right to keep what I discuss confidential *
> - I have the right not to feel judged
> - I have the right not to answer personal questions
>
>   *unless what I say is causing concern and needs to be shared

Figure 7.1 Rules of engagement

All hands up cold calling

This technique instructs all students to raise their hands whether they know the answer or not. The aim is to generate energy and participation, with all students paying attention and being keen to contribute. Would this be effective in PSHE lessons? Could it be modified?

Anonymous participation

Students are given a slip of paper or they can respond online if you are using software that allows this, e.g. Mentimeter, and asked to participate by writing a comment, view or answer. This is completely anonymous, meaning that the student does not need to worry about peer group reaction or being the focus of attention. This method can be very useful for consulting with students about sensitive or controversial topics. Would this be effective in PSHE lessons? Could it be modified?

Anonymous participation lends itself more easily to PSHE. This method can be very useful for consulting with students about sensitive or controversial topics.

The teacher can view and respond to the responses, either straight away or in the next session. This can be useful for planning or modifying PSHE lessons as you will be able to gauge student knowledge, views and anything else you asked the group to respond to.

Strategies for encouraging attention and participation are essential. However, it may be necessary to take a more nuanced approach in PSHE.

If done effectively and in line with agreed ground rules, active participation in PSHE can help assess student knowledge and skills development. I once watched a teacher assess knowledge of a term's PSHE work on unhealthy relationships and grooming using a circle time style activity. A foam ball was thrown between students and back to the teacher, and questions were posed to the students about what they had been learning. Every student was involved, and responses were rapid and exciting. The right to pass was made clear at the start of the session, but everyone fully participated. The class was engaged and knowledgeable, and had fun. They also demonstrated respect for each other and their teacher. The class were in Year 8, so 12–13 years old, and this activity may not work as effectively with older students; as a teacher, you will be able to make that call.

Lowering the stakes to encourage challenge

PSHE is not an examined subject, and it shouldn't be. It is a vital curriculum area and can support the academic curriculum. In terms of student well-being, navigating relationships and behaviour choices, the stakes could not be higher. However, it is not a high-stakes subject concerning academic performance. This allows for greater freedom in lessons, enabling students to take learning risks they may be worried about taking in other subjects. PSHE lessons also allow teachers to encourage and practise strategies that will be beneficial in other areas of the curriculum.

Inspection will examine how ambitious a setting's PSHE programme is as part of the wider personal development strand, and a PSHE programme can and should be challenging. Foundations laid in primary school and the early part of secondary school should be developed as part of a progressive programme that becomes increasingly more challenging and student led. There are many opportunities for teachers to take on a facilitation role, providing minimal input and handing learning over to students via well-constructed, active learning opportunities. In effect, students are moving from a guided learning approach to a much lighter touch and, eventually, to independence and autonomy.

This aligns with Allison and Tharby's principles of excellent teaching (cited by Clark, 2024) and applies to any subject area. However, the lower academic stakes in PSHE make it a perfect environment for students to build confidence in their ability to move from dependence to guidance and then to autonomy in their learning.

Low stakes, high challenge - An example

The lesson pack accompanying this chapter includes 30 minute activity tasking students with investigating, discussing and presenting their ideas on 'what makes a man'. The focus of the lesson pack is misogyny and this activity challenges students to consider the influences on boys and men from a range of sources including societal, family, online and more. The lesson pack is suitable for all ages and this activity is complex and multi-faceted even for older students. However, it doesn't matter if students get confused, make false assumptions or don't understand some of the content. The important feature of the activity is discussion, listening, respecting different views, and opening their mind to the multitude of influences that shape people, in this case boys and men.

Many of the theories you have studied and may be using in your specialist area will apply to PSHE. However, some will not be such a good fit, and I urge you to consider the precise aims of PSHE when deciding on the learning strategies you plan to use.

High expectations, desirable difficulty, self-regulation and connections

We should have high expectations of students' progress in PSHE, just as in any other subject. It is not an academic subject in the traditional sense, but there are clear connections between some PSHE topics and the core curriculum, which some students may find academically challenging. For example, students regularly report that they would like more finance, budgeting and taxation lessons under the broad heading of 'life skills'. This includes basic mathematical skills, and we know that many students struggle with maths and lack confidence in the functional maths skills necessary for everyday life. PSHE lessons may provide a less pressured space to approach some topics that some students may find challenging.

Emotional regulation

Self-regulation is a valuable skill, and social and emotional learning acknowledges its importance in learning and supporting emotional well-being. PSHE lessons provide a perfect environment to both explore and practise self-regulation, and the benefits of improvements will be felt widely both within and outside of school. Self-regulation can be challenging for many young people as they move through adolescence, and factors external to school play a significant role. However, high-quality PSHE can have a tremendous impact in giving students a range of strategies to help them understand and manage their emotions healthily, allowing them to self-regulate.

Teacher as a role model

The teacher's role as a role model is fundamental in this process. Facilitating lessons with emotional intelligence and empathy will engender students' feelings of belonging and help them to thrive. More than anything, this will make your PSHE programme high quality and positively impact your students.

Your high expectations regarding how they will mature and progress will foster a sense of belonging and being heard that reaps rewards within PSHE, the broader curriculum and beyond.

Top tips for being a great role model

- Be balanced but professional when listening to arguments
- Make the space and students feel safe
- Read the room

- Listen, even if student comments don't make sense or are inflammatory
- Know when to close the discussion
- Encourage reluctant students – 'You made a great point earlier; what do you think of this?'
- Respect other's viewpoints, but don't be afraid to tell students that some points of view could be illegal, go against the school ethos or be offensive
- Show that you care
- Be prepared to show vulnerability – you don't have all the answers, no-one does, so admit it
- Quality not quantity. If a discussion is going well and students are gaining a lot from it, don't move on to the next topic. Fully explore the one you are on
- Be an advocate in the staffroom. Behave in the way you are encouraging your students to behave
- Be brave enough to use different pedagogy in PSHE
- Draw from students to help them come to their own conclusions, e.g. making safe choices
- Have humility. Even if you're only 23, a 14-year-old will not see you as being part of their world

The power of connections

Connection is an area that inspectors have been discussing increasingly, and there are many reasons to focus on how topics and themes within subject areas connect. Supporting students in identifying and making connections fosters deeper learning. Recognising connections across the curriculum makes learning more relevant, especially in PSHE. For example, if you are facilitating an alcohol session, there are numerous connections to other topics within the PSHE curriculum. You can challenge students to suggest connections, which can help evaluate knowledge as students progress through school. You would expect them to identify the impact on health, legislation, societal costs, mental health, comparisons with other substances, links to crime, and relationship problems. The list goes on.

This non-siloed approach encourages curiosity and challenge, and if practised within the safe space of PSHE lessons, it may provide the confidence for students to apply this approach in other subjects.

A different interpretation of 'the lecture'

Throughout adolescent brain development, the influence of adults often becomes less important as peer approval becomes the trump card. Adults' advice from teachers and parents can be perceived as 'lecturing', no matter how gentle, understanding, and well-meaning the intention. The resulting eye-roll, or worse, sometimes tests even the most effective adult self-regulation. The 'remember I'm the adult' mantra must often be on hand!

Eventually, this will pass, but according to experts, it usually happens around age 24, so chances are you will not experience the benefits of your efforts.

Some students may be dismissive; they might think that PSHE is pointless, feel that you know nothing about what they are experiencing, and won't listen to or 'hear' what you are saying. This will be underscored if they pick up on teachers not taking PSHE lessons seriously, as discussed in Chapter 5.

To avoid 'lecturing' here are some behaviours to avoid with your students:

1. *Wholesale instruction about not doing something.* 'Don't drink until you're 18'. 'Don't smoke'. 'Vaping is bad for you'. They will already know that these are unhealthy behaviour choices, and your telling them not to engage in them will have little impact. There is always someone ready to quote that their grandparent started smoking at 12, still smokes 20 cigarettes a day, and is now 85 and healthy. Population-based health statistics are of little interest to teenagers.

2. *Avoid catastrophising.* 'Many young people carry knives, and this means they are more likely to be stabbed'. This is frightening and untrue – very few young people carry knives. However, because it is also the type of sensational comment made by the press, it could have the opposite effect to the one you want.

3. *Scare tactics can backfire.* 'Uploading an indecent image will result in prosecution and being placed on the sex offenders register'. Some students may have uploaded an image, and this action has no consequences in many circumstances, although we never want students to do this. By making statements about the worst-case scenario, even when theoretically it can happen, students may dismiss this as being untrue or 'can't happen to them'.

In summary, don't use fear to try and manage behaviour. A better approach is to provide activities that allow students to come to their own conclusions by assimilating facts and engaging in discussion. If your students have completed questionnaires reporting behaviour, sharing this with them will make the session more relevant and enable them to appreciate the myths surrounding teenage behaviour and realise that most of their peer group make safe and healthy choices. Accepting this is protective and leads to more students rejecting the behaviours they mistakenly believed many of their peers are engaging in.

Here are a few suggestions:

1. *Case studies* describe young people around the same age as your students who are experiencing a situation that requires the class to discuss and provide advice to share with the subject of the case study.
2. *What happens next?* Working in groups, the class is given some information and asked to suggest what happens next. Suggestions are fed back before the answer is provided. This type of activity can involve multiple characters and steps. Older students can consider it from the perspective of different individuals.
3. *Fly on the wall.* Use a video as a stimulus to show the manipulation of young people in some way. A good example is how companies target children and young people with unhealthy products, including vapes and alcohol.

CASE STUDY

The case study in Chapter 3 discusses the benefits of active teaching methods, which complements this chapter.

KEY TAKEAWAYS

Acknowledge that not all teaching and learning strategies will apply to PSHE.

Accept that a lecture-style format is ineffective, and students are likely to reject advice in the form of a lecture.

Aspire to include challenges in PSHE that encourage curiosity, include desirable difficulty and connect PSHE topics and broader curriculum areas, and be a great role model!

PERSONAL REFLECTIONS

1. Can you recall experiencing a lecture-style learning experience with limited learning opportunities.

2. How could you connect PSHE to your specialist subject area/s?

3. Think about the teaching strategies you use outside of PSHE, which could be effectively applied to PSHE lessons, and which would you avoid?

FURTHER READING

Clark, J (2024) *Teaching One Pagers, Evidence-informed Summaries for Busy Educational Professionals*, John Catt from Hodder Education

Lemov, D (2021) *Teach Like a Champion 3.0:63 Techniques that put Students on the Path to College*, Jossey-Bass

LESSON PACK

Misogyny, choices and consequences. This lesson pack accompanies the CPD resources that support Chapter 5. The target age group is 12-14; however, the material is suitable for all ages, including post-16 students. There are over 2 hours of activities aimed at understanding the drivers of misogyny, its impact on girls and women and the tactics used to sell misogynistic rhetoric. The materials, teacher CPD and supporting notes encourage an approach that does not 'lecture' or alienate boys.

RESOURCES

Tackling inequality

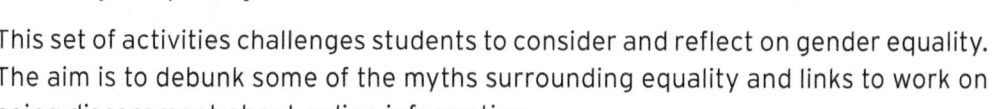

This set of activities challenges students to consider and reflect on gender equality. The aim is to debunk some of the myths surrounding equality and links to work on being discernment about online information.

The activities can be used with any age group from age 11. There are opportunities to extend or simplify the material to meet the needs of your students. The focus is on gender equality. However, taking an approach that does not create a 'them' and 'us' dialogue is essential. Various methods are used, all of which are student-focused and 'teacher-talk' is restricted to a facilitation role.

Both interpretations of 'spare me the lecture' should be apparent:

- There is variety with minimal teacher input
- Learning is through discovery, discussion and debate.

This material also links effectively to the 'Misogyny, causes and consequences' library pack, which examines the subject while taking an approach that should not alienate boys. There is also a link to accredited training to support knowledge and understanding of the best approach to deliver this topic.

The session is split into three parts and designed to take approximately 30-40 minutes. However, it could be shortened by focusing on just one of the activities.

Begin the session by sharing the ground rule that you have agreed as a class to ensure a safe and respectful learning environment.

Activity 1 - Where in the world?

The first activity introduces gender equality by asking students to discuss where they think there is the most gender equality (by country).

It is helpful to ensure that students know what gender equality is. Ask the class to suggest what they understand about gender equality and agree on a definition. Share the United Nations definition.

The United Nations defines gender equality as:

> The equal rights, responsibilities, and opportunities of all people, regardless of their gender:
>
> - **Equal rights**: Women and men, and girls and boys, have the same rights.
> - **Equal responsibilities**: Women and men, and girls and boys, have the same responsibilities.
> - **Equal opportunities**: Women and men, and girls and boys, have the same opportunities

Working in small groups task the class with:

- Discussing and noting the top 10 countries that enjoy the greatest level of gender equality
- After a few minutes, provide the following clues to help the class refine their lists:
    - Clue 1 – all 10 countries are in Europe
    - Clue 2 – the UK is not included in the top 10
    - Clue 3 – Scandinavian countries take the top three spots
- Give the class another few minutes to consider their choices and then share the top 10.

Top 10 countries for gender equality

1. Iceland
2. Denmark
3. Norway
4. Finland
5. Sweden
6. Germany
7. Lithuania
8. Belgium
9. Switzerland
10. Luxembourg

Copyright material from Angela Milliken-Tull (2025), *What Students Want From Their PSHE In Secondary School*, Routledge.

Briefly discuss the list. Are there any surprises? Can the class suggest any common features amongst the countries on the list?

- All are in Europe and the more northern parts of the region. Eight out of the 10 are in the European Union (Switzerland and Norway are not).
- The following two countries on the list are also in Europe: Austria and the Netherlands.

The top-ranking non-European country comes in next at number 13. Can the class suggest which country it is? *Clue:* it is not in Europe but in the Southern Hemisphere. It is *New Zealand*.

Ask the class if they are surprised about any countries not featured on the list. Where do the think the UK, USA and Canada appear?

> **How do the UK, USA, Canada and the Republic of Ireland rank (out of 146 countries)**
>
> - Ireland
> - Canada
> - UK
> - USA
>
> (*Source: Forbes, 2024*)

Note: The list of the countries with the greatest levels of gender parity combined how the country ranked across five global indexes and other factors, including maternity and paternity leave, maternity allowance and payments.

Activity 2 – What makes a country more equal?

Having gained some insight into the countries that have more gender equality, the next step is to understand the factors that are in place to give these countries the top scores.

Share the suggestions in Figure 7.2 and ask the students to select the features that make a country more equal regarding gender equality.

Give the group a few minutes to discuss their choices and then share the answers (see Figure 7.3).

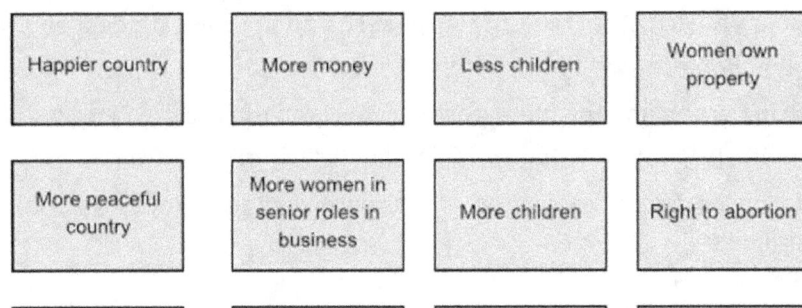

Figure 7.2 What makes countries more equal?

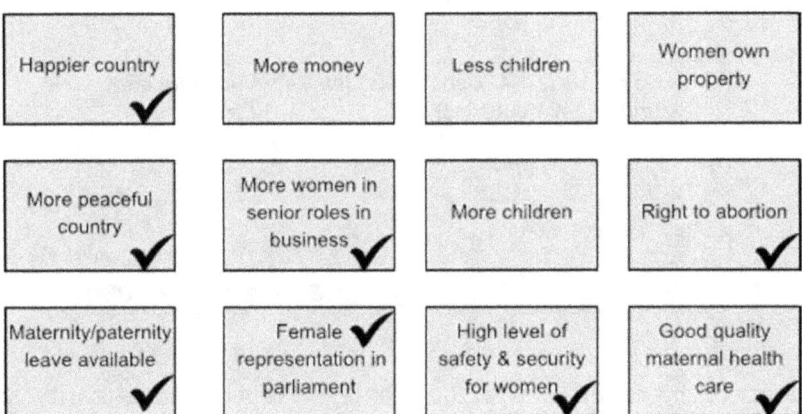

Figure 7.3 This is what makes countries more equal

Activity 3 – What can make societies more equal?

Some of the key factors that countries with a high level of gender equality exhibit include: education, employment, financial inclusion, cell phone use, parliamentary representation, absence of legal discrimination, access to justice, maternal mortality ratio, son bias, domestic violence, community safety, political violence targeting women, and proximity to conflict.

Share the information with the class and then ask them to discuss the following question (Figure 7.4): what can we learn from countries where there is more equailty? Give time for discussion and making notes and then ask each group to share their suggestions.

To conclude this session, summarise using the points below.

Designing a more equal society

How can the UK (or the country you are based in), improve gender equality?

Consider the following:

- Education to encourage mutual respect between boys and girls
- Greater representation of women in senior roles
- Breaking down stereotypes to encourage women into engineering, science and technology
- Supporting women to return to and develop their careers when they have children.

Think about the countries that do this best?

Iceland, Denmark, Finland, Norway, Sweden

What can be learned from them?

Figure 7.4 How to design a more equal society

Summary

Although some countries are doing well in reducing gender inequality, this does not mean that they have reached a situation where there is gender parity. According to the World Economic Forum (2024), reaching that goal will take more than 100 years.

Being more equal is good for society. Countries with the highest gender parity also tend to be happier, more peaceful, more democratic, healthier and more prosperous.

Extension ideas

Having considered the countries that demonstrate a high regard for gender equality, you could compare these with the areas where the opposite is the case. The best-known example is Afghanistan, where the rights of girls and women have been severely eroded. However, the indexes used to gather the data used to measure this don't include all countries, usually because they do not have systems in place to gather information.

Which countries are making forward strides towards equality? There are some countries making progress more quickly than others.

Which countries have slowed or appear to be going backwards? One of the key indicators is the right to abortion, and some countries, most notably the USA, have curtailed this right.

Copyright material from Angela Milliken-Tull (2025), *What Students Want From Their PSHE In Secondary School*, Routledge.

You may also wish to consider additional questions about equality, such as those related to LGBTQ, disability, age and race.

Individuals may be impacted by various factors that make discrimination more likely. With older students, you can consider intersectionality, probably leading to a more complex debate as the nuances and sometimes contradictions around equality are exposed. However, starting from the base of gender equality and laying the foundations is an essential first step.

8 This is so embarrassing!
Managing student and staff embarrassment in PSHE

We can't escape the fact that some topics within PSHE are embarrassing. Teachers worry about delivering sensitive or controversial material, and students are concerned about how their peers view or judge them.

This chapter will explore the root causes of some awkward moments that can arise in PSHE and how to minimise embarrassment and maximise learning.

Student embarrassment

As discussed in Chapter 4, the changes during adolescence have many ramifications, including trying to discover self-identity and feeling emotions much more strongly. Peer approval becomes far more essential, and a side effect for many is that they quickly become embarrassed.

Researchers believe that, however painful, embarrassment is an important emotional state and, as it's often related to personal or social mistakes, it can provide internal feedback that helps minimise this happening again. However, the impact of embarrassment and accompanying physiological responses such as blushing or stammering can result in negative thoughts or behaviour.

In the case of teenagers, this is often heightened, and embarrassment can result from compliments or even thoughts about how others may have perceived them. Some empathic individuals can experience embarrassment on behalf of others, and neurodivergent individuals may have more profound experiences. Despite the strength of feeling that embarrassment can elicit, including that everyone is noticing and commenting on what someone is doing or wearing and making judgements, most of the time, no one will notice.

Do all teenagers experience embarrassment to the same extent?

Although most people are likely to experience embarrassment at some point, not everyone is affected to the same extent. Some will feel profound shame if they have made a mistake or said something that breaks a social norm and is disapproved of by their peer group. Anyone suffering from social anxiety is often susceptible to more extreme embarrassment and may take steps to avoid situations where they may feel vulnerable or susceptible to embarrassment.

Individuals who laugh off embarrassing experiences are often viewed as more trustworthy and likeable. Using humour to overcome embarrassment is a good strategy.

Here are some embarrassing moments that teachers and university students have shared about embarrassing memories from their school days.

> In a sex education lesson, the teacher asked if we had any questions, I asked what an organism was. The class erupted in laughter, and I felt so humiliated and embarrassed, I wanted the ground to open and swallow me.

> The maths teacher was reading everyone's mark in a multiple-choice quiz. He told the class that a blindfolded monkey with a pin could have got a better result than me. I was embarrassed every time I was in that class from that day forward.

> I had just started at secondary school and I was one of the smaller students. My uniform was too big and my skirt was long. One of the older boys commented to his friends that mini-skirts were back in fashion. Of course, they all laughed, and I turned bright red. It wasn't a great start to secondary school.

> I suffered from acne and during one particularly nasty flare-up, a boy I had a huge crush on asked if I should be at school with chicken pox.

What embarrasses teenagers the most?

Adults, including teachers and parents, are a significant source of embarrassment. Sorry, teachers, if you are or have been a parent of teenagers, you will be very familiar with this. Younger colleagues might have more recent memories of their own experience of this.

Around the age of 13, many teenagers will no longer want to spend time with their parents in public, and at home they will spend more time in their own space. Teenagers are biologically programmed to separate from their parents as they develop their own identities. A curious manifestation of this need is a young person turning away from an activity or interest they previously shared with a parent. The teenager no longer wants this connection, and it's all part of the need to form a separate identity. Given time, this is likely to pass, and parents and children will enjoy shared activities again, but it may take some time.

As their teacher in a setting with expected behaviour norms, rules and boundaries in place, you are less likely to experience the worst of this behaviour, particularly given the all-important focus on how peers view them. Nonetheless, there may be times when you get a distinct impression that you are unimportant, embarrassing or don't 'get' them. This may be exacerbated in PSHE lessons, and it's important to remember that reactions are likely to be due to the complexities of managing self-identity and the discomfort that can often result from navigating these changes.

Embarrassment and self-consciousness, finding adults 'cringe' and needing space are all signs of normal development. However, it is still vital for teenagers to observe boundaries and be respectful. Giving some leeway is good, but there should be no excuse for rudeness in school.

Strategies for managing teenage embarrassment

Take what they say seriously

Part of adolescence is letting others, including parents and other significant adults, see the people they are becoming. This helps teenagers open up and be more willing to discuss their views. Talking down to them or being patronising – how younger children are often communicated with – is more likely to make them irritated and withdrawn.

Consider the world from a teenage perspective

Teenagers can sometimes come across as being 'know-it-alls'; however, it's important to allow the time to think through ideas and concepts, even if they are incorrect. Rather than tell them they are wrong, try responses such as 'Tell me more about that' or 'I heard something different. What do you think?' And if you are ready for a challenge, teach them *how* to think by asking what someone who disagrees with them might say and why.

Recognise when space is needed and be patient

Sometimes, teenagers need some space to process thoughts or regulate emotions. Look for the warning signs of when it's best not to push for a response or contribution.

Giving some feedback to your students to acknowledge that you recognise that they are becoming more independent and respect their new sense of identity will help them connect better with you. As brain development continues, they will gradually start to see that they are not a species entirely different from the adults in their lives, including their teachers.

Activities to help minimise embarrassment in PSHE lessons

Do	Don't
• Think about who is in your class and speak to students in advance who may be affected by content • Use ground rules at beginning of lesson • Provide a range of different activities • Allow small group and paired discussion • Consider opportunities to draw/doodle • Have a question box available • Move around the class observing and listening to discussion • Adapt activities to the group • Be present in the lesson and role model skills, e.g. active listening • Facilitate more than teach • Use distancing techniques e.g. case studies, scenarios	• Select individuals to answer questions • Use activities that the class will be uncomfortable with, e.g. role play • Ask groups or pairs to feedback discussion to the class if they are not comfortable to do so • Share personal experiences or anecdotes • Scoff or laugh at student views, opinions, even if they are incorrect • Underestimate how sensitive and easily embarrassed teenagers can be • Forget to refer back to the agreed ground rules throughout lessons if required

When teachers get it wrong

Too personal – Using yourself as a case study!
Sometimes, teachers get it wrong when trying to connect with teenagers. As the 'out of touch adult', it can be challenging to demonstrate that we understand what they are going through. A particularly 'cringe-worthy' example of this was when a member of the senior leadership team was leading an assembly for 14-15-year-olds on healthy romantic relationships. She mistakenly believed that sharing her problematic relationship and recent divorce would be a good case study. The students became increasingly uneasy as this tale of woe continued, culminating in the unfortunate teacher becoming so upset that she was escorted from the assembly hall in tears.

The story spread like wildfire throughout the school, with a range of views from students on this relationship story, not all sympathetic. Years later students were still talking about the incident.

Sharing personal information is usually unwise and risks embarrassing students at best or leading to personal ridicule at worst. Students sometimes ask teachers about their personal experiences, and it is helpful to include in your ground rules that personal questions will not be answered.

Encouraging students to support your personal views

Most teachers are passionate about education and often have other interests that they are also passionate about and hold strong views on. However, it is important when delivering PSHE lessons to be balanced. There are countless examples of the actions of well-meaning teachers resulting in problematic unintended consequences. One example was where a teacher encouraged a group of students to join her on an extinction rebellion protest. The protest became rowdy, students got frightened and parents complained to the school. Teachers have also found themselves at the sharp end of parental complaints when supporting LGBTQ+ sessions, usually when parents have not had advance warning about external visitors. This particular issue can often unfairly escalate, despite coming from a very well-intentioned place.

Engaging in gossip

Most teachers take great care to present a professional persona and do not engage in gossip. However, there are occasions where a slip-up by a teacher or student has had serious ramifications. Teachers sometimes let their guard down a little with post-16 students and this can inadvertently lead to a blurring of boundaries which can make gossip more likely. To avoid embarrassment for everyone it is always best to shut down students sharing gossip with you immediately and keep your own conversations within professional boundaries. Take care not to be overheard by students if discussing anything that could be construed as gossip or personal information when speaking to colleagues.

Teacher embarrassment

Some teachers don't like teaching PSHE because it is embarrassing. There are a range of reasons behind this, which include:

- Lack of training/CPD
- Insufficient knowledge about topics

- Religious views
- Personal experiences
- Worried about having to answer questions
- The belief that students will know more than they do about some subjects
- Fear of saying the 'wrong' thing
- Accidentally using incorrect terminology

These are all valid concerns. However, most can be quickly addressed with some staff training and ongoing support from the PSHE lead.

The importance of CPD

As discussed throughout, most teachers will have received little training on PSHE during initial teacher training. However, many will be expected to deliver lessons during time-tabled sessions or tutor time. Few schools have a specialist PSHE team, meaning that in many cases, most of the teaching team must have competence in delivering PSHE.

The topics that cause the most anxiety tend to be the more sensitive or controversial areas. Sex and relationship education tops the chart for embarrassment; however, this represents a relatively small part of the PSHE curriculum and lots of relationship education is not about intimate relationships. Nonetheless, this is the area where CPD is most often required. With good quality resources that include teacher notes and some training, most teachers should feel well equipped to facilitate relationships and sex education lessons.

Quality, up-to-date resources

Good resources, some training sessions and effective use of ground rules will address most of the bullet points above and help ensure that staff members play the all-important role of being good role models for students and demonstrate that they take PSHE lessons seriously. However, there are a few situations that may require a different approach.

What if a teacher can't or won't deliver a topic?

In cases where the teacher's embarrassment or discomfort is because of personal or religious views, it may be more difficult for that staff member to fully engage with delivering PSHE content that contradicts firmly held personal views. In this circumstance, the best course of action could be to use a different teacher for this content. Students are unlikely to receive high-quality lessons; the teacher may avoid some of the content and there is a danger that the class will conclude that the teacher is not taking the session seriously. As discussed in Chapter 5, staff role modelling provides a powerful message and one that we don't want to dilute.

This is a further area where staff CPD can be very helpful in building confidence. There is an expectation that teachers both understand and promote the Equality Act 2010 and pass this knowledge and behaviour on to students. However, within the characteristics protected by the Equality Act, some individuals may need help reconciling some of the characteristics protected if they are at odds with deeply held personal, cultural or religious views or teachings. Ultimately, legislation trumps personal views; however, recognising the complexities that can arise for some and having training to support teachers in this area will benefit students.

Top five tricky PSHE topics

When PSHE leaders survey teams to gather teacher confidence levels and interest in delivering PSHE, the results consistently fall into the following categories. The bell-shaped curve is as applicable here as in many other situations.

A relatively small number of teachers report that they are comfortable and confident in delivering PSHE lessons and are happy to do so. At the other extreme, there as teachers who state that they have no interest in PSHE or desire to be involved in this curriculum area. The majority sit in the middle ground, where they are willing to contribute but are not confident or comfortable delivering all content within PSHE.

Teachers regularly cite the five topics below as the subjects they feel most uncomfortable delivering:

1. Gender diversity, sexuality, transgender (LGBTQ+)
2. Pornography
3. Sexual harassment, assault, abuse
4. Female genital mutilation (FGM)
5. Sexual health, including sexually transmitted infections (STIs), contraception, and termination of pregnancy

Parents

Many teachers are also concerned about how parents will react to some of the content within the PSHE curriculum, which can impact confidence. Not surprisingly, the topics in the list above are also the areas where parents can be the most concerned. Although most parents are very supportive of the role school plays in educating their children about relationships and sex education, a minority have more concerns.

There are also some campaign groups with strong views about relationships and sex education who often feel very negatively about topics being covered in school, despite this being a statutory responsibility that schools are obliged to adhere to. Despite having limited support amongst the general population, these groups are often well organised and have successfully shared their views in the media and gained the support of a few MPs.

Understandably, this only adds to the anxiety that teachers and school leaders may feel about content that is already a concern for some. I always recommend that schools regularly consult with and inform parents about PSHE content. This prevents them from being blindsided. Ideally, parents should have opportunities to view material in school with a teacher explaining the rationale. Parents can also request access to teaching resources, and in this scenario, it is better to provide 'view only' content. There have been a few instances where PSHE resources have been misrepresented or taken out of context and shared via various media channels, causing embarrassment to the school.

Answering tricky questions or comments

One of the biggest worries for many teachers is about how to address questions or comments made by students in PSHE lessons. This area is where a little training and an opportunity to practise in advance can quickly alleviate fears.

Top tips for answering tricky questions:

- Use the ground rules
- Admit it if you don't know something
- Have a question box
- Think in advance about what might come up
- Practise how to answer questions

- Challenge home/pupil values with facts, legislation (Equality Act 2010) and school values

Here are some of the questions that teachers often ask about answering questions and comments with some suggestions about how to respond.

'Do I have to answer a question if it's personal?'

Some suggested responses are:

> That's about my personal life, and we've already agreed not to discuss personal information. Remember the ground rules we agreed on? Let me remind you.

> We've agreed not to make personal comments about another class member, including me or any other teacher. Remember what our ground rules say about respect.

There may be times where you want to deflect personal questions, but if the comment is valid, there may be opportunities to signpost the students to find out more:

> I'm not going to answer that from a personal perspective, as we've already set ground rules to protect our privacy. However,

> I've read about . . .

> There was a news story you might want to look at . . .

> A recent documentary covers this issue . . .

'Do I have to answer a question if it's asked?'

You are not obliged to answer questions if you don't know the answer or it is personal or inappropriate. It might be a perfectly reasonable question but not age-appropriate or about something that is not the responsibility of the school to cover. You should also be alert to questions that may indicate a disclosure or highlight a need for more specialist advice or support. For example if a student said: 'If somebody was worried about . . . where would they go for advice?', Could this be a safeguarding red flag?

It's helpful to have some responses to quickly close down questions that you are not going to answer.

> That's a fair question, but I don't think it's appropriate that we talk about it now.

That's an interesting comment, but it's not something we will learn about this week/year. (You might indicate that it will be covered at a later date.)

That's a good question but I think it's something that you should talk to your parents about.

'Do I have to answer a question immediately?'

It's not always appropriate to answer a question immediately and you may not know the answer or even fully understand what the student is asking. There are some responses you can use that will help in this situation:

That's a great question, but you'll have to give me a minute or two to think about the best way to answer that.

That's an excellent question, but rather than talk to the whole class, I'd like to see you at the end of the lesson to discuss this.

That's a fascinating comment; I'm going to go away and think about it and come back to you in our next lesson.

That is a brilliant question; I've no idea! How could we find out?

Good question: write it down and put it in the question box. Does anyone else have something they would like to ask? We can carry on our discussion next time.

'How can I buy time before answering a question?'

If a question or comment comes up that you want to answer but need a little thinking time, there are some easy ways to buy time before responding.

This is often useful when discussing topics where some students may have strong opinions. An example of this is misogyny, which was discussed in Chapter 6, but there are other topics where students may hold polarised opinions. Drug education regularly prompts comments about the legal position of cannabis; some students may have views about the age of consent being higher or lower. These discussions can be rich and insightful if facilitated well, and often the class will 'police' themselves effectively if you have given them the skills to 'agreeably disagree'.

Sorry, can you repeat that? I'm not sure I heard you correctly.

That's interesting; tell us a bit more about what you mean . . .

Hmmm, that's interesting; what do other people think?

What's another view on that?

Why might somebody else (dis)agree with that?

In summary, discussing and responding to questions and comments confidently will enhance PSHE for your students and thinking things through in advance will help manage this part of lessons effectively.

The following questions are a helpful summary when considering tricky questions and comments:

- Why is the pupil asking this question? Are there any safeguarding issues?
- Do I need to answer this question?
- Do I have to answer this question – now?
- What is the school policy on answering student's questions?
- Are there any *faith, cultural or religious sensitivities* to be considered?
- Does this pupil have *needs or circumstances* that might influence their need to ask this question?
- How best to reassure the student(s) and *identify a trusted adult*?

And remember, you do not have to answer any question you do not feel is appropriate to answer!

CASE STUDY

This case study is anonymous to avoid any embarrassment for the school discussed. It's an example of how important it is to have a well-planned and fully-embedded PSHE programme and reliance on 'off-timetable' PSHE days can lead to embarrassing results for staff and students.

Newly qualified teacher, high-performing single-sex school, England

As a newly qualified teacher, I was looking forward to teaching PSHE as I have always known what an important part of the curriculum it is and felt that I missed out in school by not being taught PSHE properly. I had also worked with a PSHE company, helping to draft lessons, which further contributed to my appreciation of the importance of this kind of education. In the school that I was working at, PSHE was taught once every 1 or 2 months as a 'PHSE day'. This meant that students had a whole day of PSHE rather then regular sessions.

Once I started to teach PSHE in my school, I quickly became disillusioned and somewhat embarrassed by the disservice I felt we were doing to the students. Firstly, doing all PSHE in one day became very boring to both the teachers and students, and they had mostly disengaged by the last few periods of the day. The teacher-taught lessons were also very brief, and we were not provided with many resources, meaning that we could quickly find ourselves struggling to fill the hour-long lesson. Not having many resources along with very long discussion times meant that teachers were often asked difficult questions that they didn't really have answers to. An example of this was when we had a year 9 lesson on periods. The session involved watching a 15 minute video, then we had a few discussion points to talk about for 25 minutes. The discussion proved difficult as despite being an all-girl setting, many students were embarrassed to contribute their points in front of the class, and we ran out of things to say. The final activity was making a poster on periods, which also seemed like a pointless time-filling activity. This lesson was particularly difficult for the male teachers who did not necessarily know a lot about this topic, and didn't have adequate training or resources to fall back on. Similar situations often arose with topics such as FGM and STIs.

As teachers can often feel slightly anxious leading lessons on these kinds of subjects, it is important to feel there is support and good quality resources in place to ease this.

Another source of embarrassment was some of the PSHE assemblies. Many school speakers do a great job and can provide a valuable contribution to the PSHE scheme. However, in my school there were a few assemblies that were not pitched at the right level or appropriate in any way, which led to embarrassment and was ultimately a waste of time and money. A particular example I remember is when the school brought in a boyband to talk about bullying. The group came in and sang some songs completely unrelated to anything to do with PSHE and talked very briefly and vaguely about bullying before proceeding to sign autographs. While this was enjoyable for the students, it did not contribute to their PSHE development, and many teachers felt embarrassed by this time-wasting activity. During the other PSHE teacher-led sessions that day, it was clear that the students hadn't learned anything about bullying and were too distracted by the boyband to focus in classes, which further contributed to the difficult position teachers were in.

Overall teaching PSHE in this school was frequently embarrassing and even 'cringe-worthy' as there was a lack of research into what should be taught and the best way of teaching it. There was also insufficient planning form the lead, which led to teachers feeling confused and unprepared for PSHE lessons, meaning that students and teachers would find themselves in awkward and embarrassing situations.

> **KEY TAKEAWAYS**
>
> *Acknowledge* that embarrassment is often an extreme and painful emotion for teenagers, but an essential part of development. Adults, especially parents, are often the cause of embarrassment in the minds of teenagers.
>
> *Accept* that teachers can feel uncomfortable and embarrassed when they feel out of control. This includes PSHE lessons on sensitive or controversial topics where there has been inadequate training.
>
> *Aspire* to PSHE lessons where embarrassment for both staff and students is minimised and learning is maximised!

> **PERSONAL REFLECTIONS**
>
> Use the following questions to help you reflect on this chapter:
>
> 1. Can you recall an embarrassing moment in your school days that has stuck with you? Have you learned anything from this experience that you applied to your teaching and student interaction?
>
> 2. Does your setting have adequate training to help staff feel confident and comfortable delivering the more sensitive PSHE content?
>
> 3. What do you think the balance should be between relationships and sex education delivered in school and parental responsibility for this content?

FURTHER READING

Hoyle, A and McGeeney, E (2020) *Great Relationships and Sex Education200+ Activities for Educators Working with Young People*, Routledge

McPhee, SL and Pugh, VM (2023) *Developing Quality PSHE in Secondary Schools and Colleges*, Bloomsbury

LESSON PACK

Students regularly report that they do not receive much PSHE education about pornography, and this is also one of the topics that teachers find potentially embarrassing.

The lesson pack to accompany this chapter provides you with approximately 2 hours of activities to help you facilitate a session about pornography. The lesson is aimed at age 13-14-year-old students and includes truths and myths about pornography, legislation, student prior knowledge, risks and dangers and quizzes to assess learning.

There are many opportunities for discussion, and informative teacher notes to support the activities.

RESOURCES

Embarrassment

Relationships and sex education is often the area of PSHE that causes the most anxiety and embarrassment for teachers. In schools where there is good communication with students about what else they would like in their relationships and sex education, students often comment on the fact that sex education is often very negative, and they would like some coverage about the more positive side of sex.

The activities below were developed with groups of teachers in England and the Republic of Ireland.

It would be essential to prepare the team to deliver this content in advance and inform parents before the lesson. The content is designed for students at the top end of school, and you will know if your students are mature enough to participate in this lesson. As a guide, it would probably not be suitable for students under 14.

Introduce the session by providing an overview of what will be covered. Explain that sex education often focuses on the negative aspects of sex such as sexually transmitted infections, unintended pregnancy, sexual assault and harassment. However, it is also essential to acknowledge that intimate relationships are a natural and positive part of life.

Give some key facts, to set the scene, including legislation, i.e. the age of sexual consent is 16.

Very few young people engage in sexual activity before the age of 16. According to the 'How Are You?' student voice survey 10% of 14-16 year olds report that they have had sex; by age 16-18 it is 25%.

Activity 1 - Why do people have sex? (10 minutes)

Take time to go over the agreed ground rules before embarking on this activity.

If your group is confident, it could work in small groups, using flipchart paper to write down as many reasons as they can think of. After a few minutes, the groups can move around the room and look at what others have written.

For a less confident group, you could give students Post-it notes and ask them to write their suggestions. Then, you can collect the notes and stick them onto flipchart paper.

This exercise would also work well using an online tool such as Mentimeter, where students could make suggestions anonymously and have them displayed as a word cloud.

Why people have sex (examples)

• To show love to their partner	• Boredom
• Curiosity	• Control
• Feel pressured	• Because it's expected
• To have a baby	• To lose virginity
• Enjoyment	• Everyone else is doing it
• To feel loved	• It's their job
• Exercise	• To avoid conflict
• Build emotional connetions	• Validation

Activity 2 – Positive and less positive reasons for having sex

This activity follows on from the first one and challenges students to separate the responses into positive and less positive reasons for having sex.

Remind students of the ground rules and be aware of your group and any potential safeguarding issues or disclosures that may arise.

Using the list prepared by the class, task the groups with deciding which reasons for having sex would be part of a healthy relationship and which are less healthy.

Follow this up by asking them to provide a definition and/or examples of active consent.

Students often comment that they spend excessive time on consent in PSHE lessons. This will establish whether they have a sound understanding of active consent.

> Active consent means affirmative, honest, conscious, voluntary, sober and ongoing agreement to participate in sexual activity.
>
> Each person involved is responsible for ensuring that there is active consent to engage in each sexual act.

This is so embarrassing! 135

Share the active consent definition with the class and ask them to discuss the following:

1. Is it essential to verbally communicate consent?
2. What non-verbal cues suggest that someone is uncomfortable with something happening to them?
3. Give examples of times when someone cannot give active consent.

Activity 3 – 'OK' or 'not OK'

This activity provides an opportunity to take a closer look at values in relation to intimacy and sexual behaviour.

Students should work in groups, and each should be given a set of cards; they must agree as a group if the statement on the card is OK or not for a student their age to experience or engage in what is written on the cards. You can add your own suggestions.

Copyright material from Angela Milliken-Tull (2025), *What Students Want From Their PSHE In Secondary School*, Routledge.

Give the groups time to discuss and make their decisions. As the activity runs, you can move around the groups to observe and listen to the discussions.

When all groups have decided what is acceptable and what is not, the class can move around the groups to compare their choices. Ask students the following question: 'How did they decide what was OK or not OK?' Expect to hear the following – not OK if it's illegal, dangerous, coercive, religious beliefs, etc.

There are some explanatory notes below about legislation.

Were there any statements where there was a consensus amongst all students?

In the plenary feedback, decisions are likely to be based on:

- Personal values
- Personal experiences
- Family background
- Cultural expectations
- Maturity

Summary

Reiterate that most young people do not have sex under 16, and the majority of 16-18 year-olds are not engaging in sexual relationships either.

There should never be any pressure to have sex.

Romantic/intimate relationships do not need to be sexual relationships.

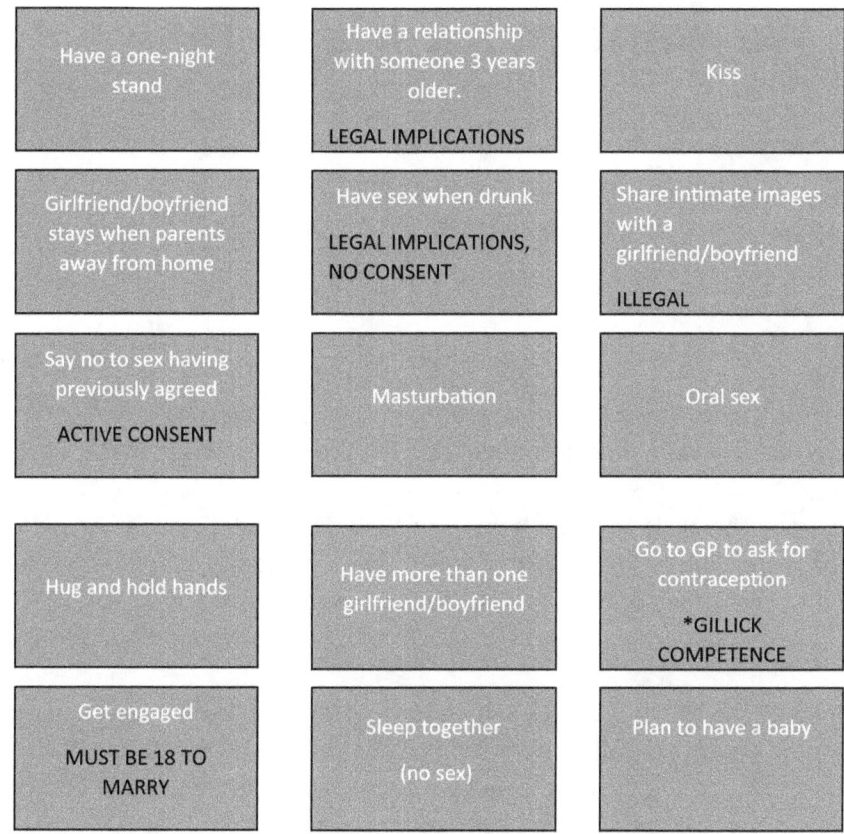

Gillick competence

Gillick competence is a medical law concept that refers to a child's ability to consent to medical treatment without parental consent. It's used when a child under 16 wants treatment, but their parents don't agree or if they want treatment without their parent's knowledge.

9   We want more life skills!

When we ask students what they want more of in PSHE lessons, the most common request is 'life skills, finance and budgeting'. In the words of a student,

> We need the skills that will help us in the adult world, such as how do I get a mortgage, what's tax, and which credit card or bank account is the best. We don't cover much of this in PSHE and it's important stuff!
>
> (Student, aged 14-16, 2023)

While much of the focus around PSHE tends to gravitate towards relationships, sex education and mental health, there tends to be far less conversation in the media and elsewhere about the more practical day-to-day skills students recognise as necessary in preparing them for adulthood.

Post-16 students ask for this content even more than their younger peers and include requests about cooking, shopping, renting a property and even doing laundry. As young people prepare for university, leaving home for a job or travelling, it is easy to overlook that they may not be fully aware of many of the everyday skills that we take for granted.

A further area that students of all ages recognise as being important is first aid. Data collected via our 'How are You?' student voice data strongly suggest that these topics are often given a 'light touch' or not covered at all.

This ties in with the persistent request for relevant PSHE and starts to give some clues about what students consider the most relevant content. When we consider the range of life skills that students regularly refer to, much of this is universally relevant and applicable to most students that you are likely to encounter. Many aspects of these topics are also far less controversial and less sensitive than some other PSHE content that teachers, parents and students can find challenging or uncomfortable. Teachers must still be provided with good quality, up-to-date resources to deliver meaningful life-skills content. We will also see that there are some connections to more sensitive content, too.

So, let's examine some of these subjects in more detail and consider how best to include them in your PSHE programme.

Budgeting, finance, money and tax

We could be forgiven for assuming that any self-respecting adolescent would be far too self-absorbed to be interested in the serious and potentially dry world of finance, budgeting and tax. However, requests for more coverage of these topics are always in the top three.

Children become aware of money from an early age, with parents most commonly the key educators about money and savings and providing context and attitudes towards money. As students get older, they become more aware of money and how much or little they have. Money is a key differentiator in many societies. When we teach about money, finance and budgeting, it is not only the facts about the cost of living, salaries, interest rates, etc., that we look at; it's also important to consider how the emotions and values associated with money affect us. We have previously discussed how brain changes during adolescence shape individuals into who they will become, as part of a journey of self-discovery and identity formation, with personal values being closely tied to money. Conversely, self-image can affect how financially successful we are likely to be (Akerlof & Kranton, 2010).

The darker side of self-identity

Over the past few years, we have become increasingly aware of the darker side of a particular type of self-identity being promoted as a route to professional and financial success. The rise of online influencers targeting boys and young men with messages depicting what their identity should be and how this will, in turn, lead to success has become very prevalent and often targets some of the most vulnerable. Intertwined with this 'recipe for success' is misogynistic rhetoric. The name most associated with this phenomenon is Andrew Tate. As a result of the arrest and the ongoing pursuit of Tate for a range of crimes, he no longer looms so large in this online space. However, there are plenty of others lining up to take his place.

The interrelationships between the many topics within PSHE are vast, and this is yet another example. The straightforward and slightly dry world of finance and budgeting soon becomes much more exciting and potentially controversial, opening discussion and debate.

Online financial rewards, empowering opportunities or exploitation?

The world of online influencers is pervasive, and more young people may be considering how they can develop a career as an influencer. For many, this is a pipe dream that will soon evaporate; however, if young people have something to offer and the time and tenacity to build a following, it may be an option for some. If successful, the financial rewards can be attractive, but the flip side of this enterprise is burn-out, fear of failure and the stress associated with constantly being on show, performing and maintaining and growing an audience. There have been examples of successful influencers dying by suicide, so we never quite know what is going on behind the camera.

The new 'career' aspirations

The other 'get rich quick' phenomenon that has become more widely known and talked about is 'OnlyFans'. This online streaming platform created in 2016 is synonymous with pornography and fetishes despite other creators also using the site for fitness videos and other non-sexual content. The platform's popularity has increased exponentially in recent years and although it is an adult site, there are concerns that under-18s are not only accessing it but also posting online to make money from explicit content.

- Most OnlyFans creators are women, but most users are men
- There has been significant growth in content between 2022 and 2024 (Statista 2024).

Some celebrities have had their contracts severed following the discovery that they have an OnlyFans account, with some reporting that they not only make a lucrative and steady income from this activity but that they are also able to present themselves more accurately and claim not to share sexually explicit content.

There are other examples of 'everyday' people having to explain themselves to their HR department upon discovering an OnlyFans presence. Whether this is due to taxation issues or on moral grounds is unclear.

How can you address this?

- Take a spiral progressive approach blending and connecting the lessons that will form foundations for more complex and controversial topics
- Build understanding on internet safety and the skills to identify online dangers

- Relationships education should include healthy online and offline relationships. Using scenarios and case studies to allow students to come to their own conclusions will help the learning to be internalised
- Be factual and non-judgemental. Introducing moral debate can be powerful if well-managed
- Include legislation pertinent to the topics being covered without using scare tactics

Renting and buying property

Whether thinking about university, training or finding a job, students' thoughts and questions often turn to what they need to know when renting or buying a property. Equipping students with the basic facts about rental contracts or mortgages can be built into PSHE lessons and links closely with budgeting and earnings. For students considering university, renting property is a crucial topic as it can be fraught with problems if not carefully thought through. Once again, parents may take on much of the responsibility in this area, but some input from the school is likely to be helpful.

How can you address this?

- Give students opportunities to work through scenarios that present real-life situations
- Feature young people in a range of different circumstances
- Present a range of budgets and options available
- Explain the types of situations they might find themselves in and, therefore, provide opportunities to prepare
- Encourage students to reach their own conclusions

Be prepared

As a teacher, it's helpful to understand and have some ideas about how you will respond to any questions or comments about online career or money-making opportunities that might come your way. With older students, there are opportunities for discussion and debate about the potentially exploitative nature of online platforms for both creators and users. You should have good quality resources to help you respond to questions; however, even with the most up-to-date material there can be a lag between a new issue emerging and the resource being updated.

Relevance and progression

Within a PSHE programme, a spiral and progressive approach to life skills education will combine knowledge about managing money and budget, possibly using pocket money as an example. Many free resources, often supplied by banks, support this. Societies worldwide are increasingly cashless, which should be a key feature when delivering lessons about money. As students move through school, more complex content can be introduced. Tax, national insurance, savings and interest rates can be built into practical activities that link to budgeting and the range of salaries associated with different job roles.

It is important to ensure that lessons and activities are relevant to your cohort by considering their next steps in further education or employment. Students often complain that there is an over-emphasis on university and less focus on other career routes. It can be helpful to use a wide range of examples and scenarios to ensure inclusivity, including for students with disabilities. Linking with your careers lead will also help connect PSHE learning about life skills with the requirements the careers team is expected to cover.

When considering education about earning and saving money, it is also helpful to include ways money can be lost. There is a vast array of dangers associated with money and finance, from criminal activities such as scams and fraud to poor decision-making, including overspending, misuse of credit cards, and gambling, to name just a few.

Lessons on finance and money can generate plenty of discussion and debate. If you are interested in philosophical discussion, you may wish to share some of the ideas from political philosopher Michael Sandel. He poses moral questions that delve into what it means for society when almost everything has a price (Sandel, 2013).

Life skills beyond money, finance and tax

Students have suggested a wide range of 'life skills' that they would like to learn, including cooking, laundry, cleaning, changing a tyre and even sewing a button on clothing. Of course, many of these basic skills are unlikely to find their way onto an already tight timetable. However, there is potential for setting students challenges to learn some of these skills from family members or using online platforms such as YouTube. Potentially, the different skills learned outside of school could be shared in a PSHE lesson. This will allow a further life skill to be practised, i.e. planning independent learning with some success criteria built in.

In an ideal world, there would be opportunities for all students to have some lessons on basic cooking and other design and technology skills. However, many schools no longer offer design and technology, meaning that these opportunities have been lost. Finding different ways to address these needs can be challenging but no less critical. As students move towards independence in young adulthood, the skills needed for practical everyday living become more pressing. Seemingly simple tasks such as preparing food without giving yourself or others food poisoning or how often bedding or towels should be washed may be a mystery for a young person who has yet to think about the mundane tasks a parent has taken full responsibility for. For many, delegation isn't easy, and we can all be guilty of completing tasks ourselves as it's easier than explaining how to do it to someone else. This can be especially true when it comes to parents and children.

First aid

Schools are often surprised when first aid appears near the top of the list of topics that students want more input on. This is usually because they have had organisations providing first aid sessions in school and assume that the bases have been covered. School visitors often provide excellent, high-quality input; however, it should be considered the icing on the PSHE cake.

A whole-school approach to PSHE and personal development with an embedded programme linking careers, citizenship, values, aspirations and connecting subjects across the curriculum will provide the strong foundations that lead to deep learning and a wide range of emerging and developing life skills. Sprinkling on the fairy dust of some interesting visitors can enhance but not replace this.

First aid, context and consolidation

So, how can we make first aid feel more embedded within PSHE?
Consider pre- and follow-up sessions for any practical input on first aid. This might include presenting students with a range of situations that they could realistically encounter, allowing them to apply knowledge and skills from practical sessions and build further knowledge.

For younger students, this could include tasking them with explaining what they would do if a friend experienced a minor or more severe injury. Examining more common situations, such as cuts, bites and stings, would be beneficial, as there is a higher chance of them happening; however, knowing what to do in more serious situations should also be included.

Older students introduce scenarios that include misuse of alcohol or other substances and explore the concerns young people may have about legal implications. A meaningful life skill is understanding the importance of seeking medical assistance and sharing information with professionals when something illegal is involved.

Time it right!

A situation where first aid knowledge or skill may be required can occur anytime. However, more injuries occur in the summer. Research from other parts of the world links higher summer injury rates to increased free time, although there is little UK-specific data on this.

Researchers from Newcastle University and Oxford University NHS Trust investigated 11,676 A&E visits for sports injuries and found that 10-14-year-olds were most likely to be injured, followed closely by the 15-19-year age group. (Hammet, 2024)

Life skills - The widest definition

Everything delivered in PSHE and PD could be described as life skills, but student interpretation is narrower. Connecting this narrower focus to the broader PSHE/PD curriculum and beyond is crucial, particularly when focusing on the skills that employers will be looking for. This includes communication, problem-solving, emotional intelligence, creativity, negotiation and more. So, as we work with students to develop the life skills that will set them up effectively for the future, consider activities to connect the wide range of knowledge and skills required for successful relationships, careers and mental and physical health alongside the values and attributes that will form their emerging self-identity.

There is further discussion of the skills employers seek in Chapter 3 alongside the role of social and emotional learning in PSHE.

CASE STUDY

Max Humpston of Global Education partners has written this case study.
With a blend of education and business experience and passion for personal development, he is in a perfect position to discuss the need for 'life skills' from a global education perspective.

How can we integrate financial literacy into the education system?

I was recently looking into investment/savings options as I start to plan financially for the future. With very little financial planning knowledge, I really didn't know where to start. The more I delved into the various options, whether it was different savings accounts, funds, equities or private pensions, the more I realised how little I actually knew.

My own cluelessness made me both anxious and really rather frustrated. I was anxious on the one hand, as I felt like I may be missing a piece of the puzzle, and perhaps should have educated myself a bit earlier, and frustrated on the other hand as I reflected on the distinct lack of education I'd actually received around this utterly fundamental aspect of life.

You'd have thought that growing up in a relatively prosperous area of the UK, going to a very good local school and even having an accountant as a father, I would know a bit about where to allocate my own finances to ensure my future wasn't a ruinous mess. You'd be wrong.

After spending hours fumbling my way through various online sites, talking to friends and family, and asking far too many questions down the phone to a poor chap from Hargreaves Lansdown, I now have a rough idea of what I should be doing, but this whole process really got me reflecting around the current state of the education system in the UK, what subjects we should be teaching more of, and how we are effectively preparing young people for their futures.

There currently seems to be a prevailing assumption that people will naturally pick up this knowledge as they grow up and enter the world of work, and that it isn't really the responsibility of educational institutions to thoroughly guide and prepare young people around such topics that may not be directly relevant to their immediate futures/exams, etc. Again, thinking back to my own experience at school, I'm finding it hard to remember having a single in-depth session on the practical implications and importance of personal finances and savings how to open a bank account, what a mortgage is, what credit is, etc.

Although often integrated within other subjects like Mathematics (with the obvious overlap being the topic of numbers), I would argue that such life fundamentals like personal finances should be a completely standalone subject. And not just for Secondary, but for Primary students too.

In-depth financial advice often comes at a cost when you're older, so the more this knowledge is freely accessible and taught in schools I think the better off we'll all be.

Having spoken to hundreds of educators all over the world the last 2 years, through building the International Schools Network, this topic has come up again and again, and I've met some people along the way doing incredible things in this space, making real headway with schools in helping students build this knowledge. One example being a recent conversation I had with the team at Squirrel (https://squirreledu.co/), who have developed a great tool for schools, helping gamify financial education, making it accessible, relatable and fun, for a broad range of ages.

And more broadly speaking, I've also come across several great free resources that hopefully may be useful for you too, especially if you're just starting out on this journey. Three are listed in the Further Reading section at the end of this chapter.

KEY TAKEAWAYS

Acknowledge that more focus on budgeting, finance, tax and first aid is likely to enhance your PSHE programme.

Accept that most students have a relatively narrow definition of what life skills are.

Aspire to build stronger connections between wider-ranging life skills that help shape personal identity.

PERSONAL REFLECTIONS

Use the boxes for your personal reflections on this chapter.

1. Do you believe that PSHE includes enough of the 'life skills' described by students, e.g. finance and budgeting?

2. Is the focus on career options too narrow? Should PSHE and career education include discussion on some of the emerging options available online, including potential dangers?

3. Does your school provide opportunities for students to acquire the skills and knowledge to manage emergency first-aid situations? Why do you think so many students report a gap in this area

FURTHER READING

Khan Academy, Personal finance, https://www.khanacademy.org/college-careers-more/personal-finance

Sandel, MJ (2013) *What Money Can't Buy: The Moral Limits of Markets*, Penguin

Resources for improving financial literacy, https://www.investopedia.com/best-resources-for-improving-financial-literacy-5091689

Guidance on money and debt, https://www.citizensadvice.org.uk/debt-and-money/

Advice from Martin Lewis, https://www.moneysavingexpert.com/banking/

LESSON PACK

To reflect the very wide range of topics that can be considered essential life skills, two lesson packs support this chapter.

Budgeting skills provide a minimum of 2 hours of activities covering saving, debt, managing a budget, the difference between wants and needs and the importance of budgeting in the adult world. These lessons include opportunities for discussion and a variety of practical exercises. The content is aimed at 14-16-year-old students.

The second resource pack is aimed at 13-14-year-olds and examines substances and emergencies. These materials could be used to consolidate learning if students have completed practical first-aid sessions, but they also can stand alone. There are at least 2 hours of activities with distanced learning techniques used to consider the situations that teenagers might encounter and the appropriate actions to take in these circumstances. What to do in an emergency includes risk assessment, safety around substances and understanding when emergency action is required.

RESOURCES

Life skills

Students want more life skills, and this set of activity delves into the types of life skills they are referring to, with follow-up activities to address these. The activities are designed to take 40–60 minutes and could be run over two shorter sessions.

Introduction and baseline assessment

Activity 1 – Ranking exercise (10 minutes)

When students were asked 'What would you like more of in your PSHE lessons?', how do you think they answered?

Provide the range of topics in Figure 9.1 and ask students to discuss in small groups or pairs which they think made it into the top five.

Rank the following topics, select the top five

Take some feedback from the groups and note the topics that are occurring most often. Share the top five from the 'How Are You?' survey of 11,000 students.

Figure 9.1 Top five life skills

Copyright material from Angela Milliken-Tull (2025), *What Students Want From Their PSHE In Secondary School*, Routledge.

Compare your student's top five with the broader data set. Are there similarities?

The top five

- First place – managing finance
- Second place – first aid
- Third place – managing relationship changes
- fourth place – mental health
- Fifth place – pornography

Activity 2 – Skills for life (20 minutes)

What are the most important skills for life?

Present this question to your class and task them with discussing the essential skills they will need as they become more independent and embark upon the next stage of their education or into work (5 minutes). Students should work in small groups.

Share the following:

• Communication	• Cooking
• Negotiation	• Car maintenance
• Problem-solving	• Household chores
• Creativity	• First aid
• Emotional intelligence	• Food shopping
• Managing money/budgeting	• Buying property
• Understanding tax	• Renting property
• Repairs (DIY/sewing, etc.)	• Self defence

Which of the skills in the table did the class include?

Which life skills are most important?

Working in groups of three, the class reads through the scenario with each group member reading one of the parts of Mia, Jake and Chloe.

Mia: I'm telling you, time management is the key to everything. If you can't organise your day, you'll never get anywhere. Between school, work and everything else, you'll drown in stress.

Jake: Time management's great, but nothing else matters if you can't manage yourself. Like how are you going to keep yourself motivated to follow your schedule if you don't even know how to push yourself to get things done?

Chloe: That's true, Jake. But you know what I think is really missing here? Money management. You can be great at time management and self-discipline, but if you don't know how to budget, save or even just avoid blowing all your cash, you'll end up struggling no matter what.

Mia: Money management, seriously? I get it, but it's not something you need to worry about right now. Once you get a job, yeah, but we're talking about life skills for right now – like, managing homework, activities and just staying on top of things.

Jake: But if you don't know how to manage money from the start, you'll make dumb decisions. Look at how many people end up in debt or living paycheck to paycheck because they didn't learn the basics when they were young. Learning to save now? That's way more useful than stressing about time management in high school.

Chloe: Exactly. You can have your perfect schedule, but if you're constantly broke or maxing out your credit cards, nothing will be easy. I know adults who can't even budget for a simple trip without stressing over it.

Mia: Okay, fair. Money management's important. But you need to know how to manage yourself first. If you can't keep yourself from procrastinating or blowing off your responsibilities, no amount of budgeting or time-blocking will save you.

Jake: Yeah, but don't you think that kind of self-discipline is part of managing money, too? If you can't control yourself when you see something you want to buy, you'll just impulse-spend and end up broke. It's all about balance.

Chloe: You two are basically saying the same thing! Self-discipline, time management and money – it's all connected. You need all of them. I still think problem-solving should be higher up on the list, though. Like, when you hit a roadblock, what do you do? Panic? Or figure it out?

Mia: Well, problem-solving definitely matters, but you can't get very far if you don't know how to plan your time or stick to your plan.

Jake: And if you can't control yourself or manage your money, you're going to hit a wall no matter how well you manage your time.

Chloe: So we all agree on one thing – life is complicated. You need time management, self-discipline, problem-solving and money management. Basically, everything.

Mia: Well, at least we can agree on that! Guess we all need to work on balancing it all, huh?

Jake: Yeah, and I'm pretty sure we'll need more than a few life hacks to pull it off.

They all laugh as the conversation turns into a more light-hearted discussion of how they can work on these skills – time management, money and everything in between. They realise that figuring out life isn't so simple, but it's a journey they'll all face.

Discuss the following questions

- Whose views do you agree with most? Why?
- Are there other essential life skills that the scenario does not include?
- Which life skills should be taught in school?
- Which life skills could you be learning in your own time?

Take some feedback from the groups. Is there a consensus on which life skills are most important?

Activity 3 – Final challenge (10 minutes)

Working individually, task students with selecting a new skill they would like to learn or improve in their own time. The template can be used to structure this. Students should draw on what they have learned in the session. It will be helpful if they have a logbook or journal to keep notes, which could be beneficial when preparing a CV or personal statement.

Something I would like to learn that will be helpful in my future is:	
What knowledge do I need?	
Where will I find it?	
What skills do I need?	
How will I practise?	
Who can help me?	
In what ways will this help me in my future?	
What else do I want to learn?	

Copyright material from Angela Milliken-Tull (2025), *What Students Want From Their PSHE In Secondary School*, Routledge.

Summary

Round up the session with the following points:

- It is important to build knowledge and develop skills
- Values and attitudes are also important, and it is the combination of all these factors that help us to move through life successfully
- Some skills will be developed in school, but many others can be learned and practised in other areas of life
- Demonstrating to admissions tutors or employers that you have been developing knowledge, skills, positive values and attitudes will be important in interviews, and it's important to keep a record of these when building a CV

10 Teacher wellbeing?
How can you stop your bucket from overflowing?

Throughout this book, the focus has been on student views and how we can better understand these findings to provide them with relevant PSHE and positively impact wellbeing.

To conclude this book, it is only right that we discuss teacher wellbeing. Recently, there has been increasing concern about the pressure on schools and teachers coming from many directions. In the discussion below, John Rees provides an overview of some of the recent findings around teacher wellbeing and explores how PSHE and work on student wellbeing can positively affect staff wellbeing.

What do we know about staff wellbeing? John Rees, Independent PSHE consultant

This book has rightly focused on improving children's and young people's wellbeing through high-quality PSHE education. This final chapter describes how the provision of the statutory expectations of relationships (and sex) and health education can improve health outcomes and support academic attainment. The links between pupils' health and wellbeing and their attainment have long been established (PHE/NAHT 2014), a notion endorsed by the chief medical officer in 2013, who described PSHE as forming a bridge between health and education by building resilience and wellbeing. She described the virtual cycle that can be achieved whereby pupils with better health and wellbeing can achieve better academically, leading to greater success (CMO 2013).

Similar expectations to improve pupils' physical and mental health and academic attainment are made clear in the introduction to the R(S)HE Guidance from the Secretary of State (DfE 2019). The potential for mutual improvement has subsequently been endorsed with evidence from the Education Endowment Foundation about the benefits of social and emotional learning, metacognition and self-regulation and, most recently, oral language interventions.

DOI: 10.4324/9781032724638-10

How can PSHE education contribute to a positive school culture and benefit staff wellbeing?

Evidence suggests that staff and pupil wellbeing is a virtuous spiral, where teacher wellbeing positively impacts pupils, so happy and healthy children learn better. Energised by children and young people who engage with learning and enjoy being a part of their school community benefits children's attainment and supports staff wellbeing.

Staff wellbeing, especially that of teachers, is a critical factor in educational effectiveness, directly impacting pupils' academic achievement and overall school experience. This relationship becomes even more critical when the education sector faces significant challenges, including workload pressures, teacher retention issues and rising mental health concerns. Understanding how teacher wellbeing affects pupil outcomes can help schools, policymakers and communities support teachers better, creating more resilient and effective educational environments.

Sadly, the most recent Teacher Wellbeing Index 2023 from Education Support (a unique UK charity dedicated to supporting the mental health and wellbeing of education staff) reveals some alarming statistics:

- 78% of all education staff report feeling stressed, a 3% increase from the previous year
- 89% of senior leaders (rising to 95% among headteachers) and 78% of teachers reported feeling stressed
- 36% of teachers reported experiencing burnout, a 9% increase from 2022

These data are mirrored in new Edurio research describing the challenges that teachers, leaders and other school staff face. Staff Wellbeing in Academies surveyed more than 11,000 education professionals across England about their wellbeing from September 2023 to March 2024. Amongst the worrying statistics, there was a silver lining: over half of teachers surveyed (54%) often feel excited about their work, demonstrating their passion and dedication. Leadership staff were even more positive, with 77% feeling excited.

What contributes to teacher wellbeing, and what reduces it?

Teacher wellbeing involves physical, emotional and professional satisfaction and balance in the lives of educators. It includes job satisfaction, manageable workloads, supportive relationships, professional autonomy and mental health. Positive wellbeing enables teachers to engage more meaningfully with their work and be more present, responsive and enthusiastic. Poor wellbeing can lead to stress, burnout and high turnover rates, which, in turn, affect educational outcomes.

High workloads and limited planning and personal development time are major teacher stressors. The intense focus on performance metrics and accountability measures has added pressure, contributing to feelings of stress and burnout among educators. According to the NFER, teacher stress in England is significantly higher than that in other professions, with 85% of teachers reporting workload as a key factor impacting their wellbeing (National Foundation for Educational Research, 2021). According to the Health and Safety Executive, teaching is among the top five occupations affected by work-related stress, with 70% of teachers and lecturers saying that their health has suffered because of their job (Labour Force Survey).

A significant aspect of teacher wellbeing is job satisfaction, which is closely linked to the perception of professional support and recognition. According to Day and Gu (2009), teachers who experience a high level of support from their peers and administration report higher satisfaction and commitment to their roles. This support fosters resilience, a critical element in managing the challenges of teaching. When teachers feel valued and recognised, they are more likely to have positive mental and emotional states, positively influencing their interactions with pupils (Day and Gu, 2009).

Teacher wellbeing is essential for teachers and significantly affects pupil outcomes. Teachers with poorer wellbeing may be less able to form strong relationships with pupils, adversely impacting the quality of teaching and the classroom environment. Conversely, teachers who maintain positive wellbeing are better equipped to create a supportive, inclusive and stimulating learning environment, which promotes higher pupil engagement and achievement.

Harding et al. (2019) suggest that teachers' mental health is strongly linked to classroom presence and attentiveness, which are crucial for facilitating effective learning. Teachers who maintain good mental health can better support pupils emotionally and academically, fostering a classroom environment that promotes positive behaviour and engagement.

Briner and Dewberry (2007) conducted a large-scale project exploring the links between staff wellbeing and school performance. Data were collected from staff in primary and secondary schools and found a significant positive association between teacher wellbeing and SATs results in primary schools, with wellbeing accounting for 8% of school performance variance. In secondary schools, they also found a significant positive association between teacher wellbeing and results at KS4 (age 16).

What is being done at a policy level to support teacher wellbeing?

Recognising the importance of teacher wellbeing, the UK government and education bodies have introduced policies to reduce stressors and enhance teacher support. Key interventions include workload reduction initiatives, access to mental health resources, and professional development programmes focusing on teacher resilience and wellbeing. Studies show that resilience training can improve wellbeing by providing teachers with tools to reframe stressful situations and maintain a healthy work-life balance.

Research by Beltman et al. (2011) indicates that teachers with resilience training report lower levels of stress and a higher capacity to cope with demanding aspects of the profession, directly benefiting their classroom engagement and effectiveness (Beltman et al., 2011).

Supportive and inclusive school culture

Creating a supportive and inclusive school culture is one of the most impactful ways to promote teacher wellbeing. When school leaders prioritise teacher wellbeing, foster open communication, and encourage a sense of community, teachers are more likely to feel valued and committed to their roles. A supportive culture that promotes collaboration, peer support, and shared responsibilities improves teacher morale and enhances pupil outcomes. Research demonstrates that a positive school climate is directly associated with higher levels of teacher wellbeing and, subsequently, higher levels of pupil achievement (Collie et al., 2012).

Unfortunately, the drive for better academic performance largely ignores these factors. Sadly, our belief in the individual's resilience has made us forget that children and adults thrive when the environments surrounding them are fully capable of facilitating their success.

Psychologists will frequently tell us that children's capacity for learning correlates directly to their capacity for relationships. There is, therefore, a moral imperative to capitalise upon the statutory expectations to teach relationships education to improve learning across the curriculum. More simply, happy, healthy pupils learn better, and this will be influenced by their capacity to understand and manage their emotions, manage their relationships, and reduce disruption, all of which should form part of the rationale for PSHE education.

Meet statutory expectations to promote staff wellbeing?

Even if we only manage to provide the statutory expectations of R(S)HE, and don't extend this to the broader expectations of PSHE education, if well taught, the expectations for children should positively impact staff. When we teach our pupils about mental wellbeing, we should be able to enable them to improve how they manage their emotions and relationships. This should lead to less disruptive behaviour and consequently support staff wellbeing. When we teach about Internet safety and harms and can improve online safety and reduce bullying and harassment, this benefits children, young people and the staff supporting them. Even teaching about puberty to improve children's awareness and self-confidence should enhance children's self-worth, which contributes to learning and staff wellbeing.

Secondary schools are also expected to improve sexual and relational health, and this can contribute to a postponement of sexual experience, reduce regret and improve contraceptive use, and therefore reduce the number of teenage pregnancies while enhancing sexual health. This can be achieved by learning about consent and reducing misogyny and discrimination; however, it also relies on developing crucial interpersonal skills. Many relationships and sex education teachers will aim for the attributes, skills, and knowledge acquired to improve intimate relationships. Developing these so-called soft skills, which numerous people seem to find quite challenging, can also enhance relationships in the dinner queue and, ultimately, employability skills.

Most educators recognise the significant contribution that PSHE can make to a positive whole school culture, which, according to Banerjee et al. (2013), can significantly improve children's attainment. Such improvements in a positive school ethos benefit all members of the school community.

In summary

The wellbeing of teachers is integral to the success of all educational settings, with far-reaching implications for student achievement, teacher retention, and overall school climate. By fostering a culture that values teacher wellbeing, schools can create learning environments where pupils thrive and teachers are more motivated, satisfied and resilient.

Supporting teachers through manageable workloads, mental health resources and CPD to provide high-quality R(S)HE/PSHE and a positive school culture benefits the staff and has a measurable impact on pupils' engagement and academic success. Given the strong link between teacher wellbeing and pupil achievement, prioritising teacher support for and of PSHE education must be a central focus in improving educational outcomes for children and young people.

Supporting teacher wellbeing – some practical suggestions

John has echoed many of the themes throughout this book, highlighting the importance of staff CPD, the benefits of an effective PSHE programme and the acknowledgement that a whole school approach to PSHE will benefit students as they move towards the next stages of their lives.

Teachers, by default, should benefit from better student wellbeing, but what else can teachers do to support their wellbeing?

Don't let your stress bucket overflow!

The stress bucket analogy, developed by Professor Alison Brabban and Dr Douglas Turkington in 2002, is regularly used to help understand both the causes of stress and strategies to help individuals cope and improve mental health and wellbeing. It is a helpful and easily understood concept.

There are a few things to consider when using this analogy.

1. Stress buckets come in different sizes. The amount of stress individuals can deal with is variable and may change over time. Let's take teenagers as an example at a population level. Most will fill their stress bucket more quickly during this time of rapid physical and emotional change compared with most adults. However, this is not a universal truth, and some young people may manage stress very well, while some adults struggle more.

2. The causes of stress are also very individual. The most stressful life events are regularly reported as bereavement, divorce and moving house, and many may agree with one or more of these events. However, you may have experienced something different.

3. A little stress is considered positive, as it can give us a sense of purpose and be motivating. However, high levels of ongoing stress are detrimental to both mental and physical health. Conversely, boredom, particularly at work, is a cause of stress. It is unlikely that, as a teacher, you are often bored at work!

4. De-stressors are also very individual, and while some might find going for a run the best way to unwind after a stressful day, others cannot imagine this to be relaxing and might prefer to lose themselves in a good book, relax in a

steaming bath, or chat with friends. The key is to identify what works for you and take time to engage in this positive and restorative behaviour.

5. False de-stressors, such as substances like tobacco and alcohol, are used by some to de-stress. While smoking has reduced considerably and does not alleviate stress (users are simply reacting to relief from nicotine withdrawal), alcohol, for many, is their 'go-to' relaxant. There can be a danger in relying on substances to relax, as it is likely that the amount of alcohol, for example, will need to increase to produce the same effect, and this can be problematic for both mental and physical health.

6. There are positive strategies to reduce stress. In addition to enjoyable relaxation forms that move focus to a stress-free place, various methods can be employed to improve positive thinking and gain perspective. One of the best-recognised is mindfulness practice. However, other strategies, including journaling and gratitude practice, can also help manage stress.

Figure 10.1 is an example of the stress bucket analogy, and at the end of the chapter, you will find Figure 10.3 as a photocopiable version that could be used individually or with colleagues. There is no reason why you couldn't use this with students too.

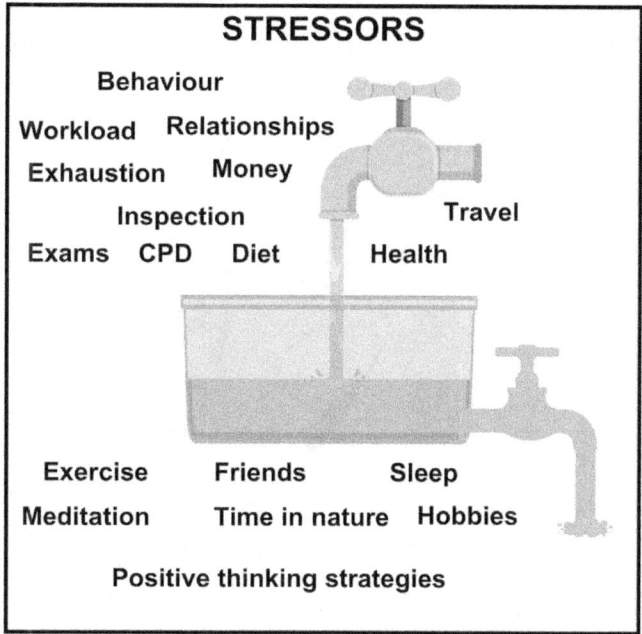

Figure 10.1 Example of stressors and ways to relax

160 *What Students Want from their PSHE in Secondary School*

If you were running a staff CPD session about managing stress you might like to try the following structure.

1. Welcome and ground rules. Just like student PSHE sessions, staff must feel that they are in a safe learning environment. Invite the group to suggest the ground rules they would like to be in place.

2. Invite colleagues to reflect on their current stress level: 'on scale of 1 to 10 how stressed do you feel?' See Figure 10.2. Some conditions can be added, e.g. in school, at home, on holiday, weekdays compared with weekends, etc. There is no need for this information to be shared.

3. Give colleagues the stress bucket template and explain the concept. Ask them to note what their stressors are and how they relax. You can use the completed example if necessary.

4. It can be helpful to divide stressors into work, personal and other categories. In a work situation it would be most appropriate to focus on stressors in the workplace.

5. The next step would be to divide the workplace stressors into topics that can be controlled and those that can't. If we are explicitly looking at stress related to PSHE, the next step would be to consider which solutions could be implemented to reduce teacher stress in this area.

6. The same principles can be used with students. Our survey results show that many students struggle to manage work and exam stress. The stress bucket model could be used to identify the specific stress points around these solutions and also consider relaxation strategies.

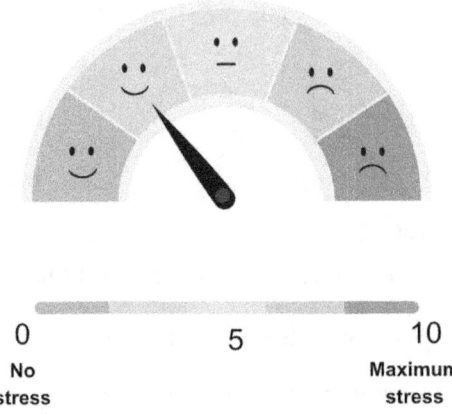

Figure 10.2 The stress scale

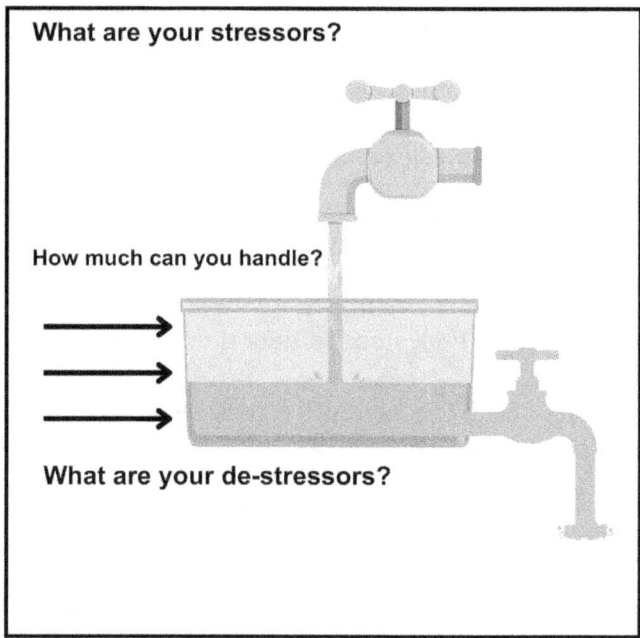

Figure 10.3 The stress bucket template

What can schools do to reduce teacher stress?

Towards the end of the COVID-19 pandemic, I was commissioned by a local authority to find out more about stress in school for both teachers and support staff. The local authority was considering funding online counselling services that staff could access. An anonymous survey was used to consult with primary, secondary and special school staff. The findings surprised the commissioners as, although respondents reported feeling more stressed and anxious, very few felt that an online counselling service was something that they would use.

The most reported issue that caused stress was a lack of work-life balance. Unsurprisingly, stress was lower when senior leadership were viewed as supportive, even if there was not much that they could do to alleviate what was causing the stress.

A significant minority of teachers reported that their experiences of teaching through the pandemic, often remotely, had led to them choosing to leave the profession. A few cited the 'invasion of privacy' that they felt when delivering lessons from home as a further example of no work-life balance.

Schools can take steps to support staff's better work-life balance with senior leadership taking the lead:

- Have a set number of days across the year for meetings to ensure staff only sometimes attend meetings at the end of the school day.
- Shared files of resources for lesson planning
- Remind staff to keep lesson plans simple; it doesn't have to be a work of art!

However, teachers can also take steps to help themselves:

- Don't be a perfectionist! Teachers often have perfectionist tendencies, trust your expertise and keep things simple.
- Don't have work emails on your mobile phone.
- Aim to complete work in school rather than take it home with you.
- Have friends who aren't teachers; otherwise, you will always be talking about school.

It is not easy to get the balance right. However, your wellbeing is important and should be a top priority!

KEY TAKEAWAYS

Acknowledge that teaching is both rewarding and challenging. Your wellbeing, as well as that of your students, should be a priority.

Accept that good enough is good enough! Aiming for perfection 100% of the time will probably lead to your bucket overflowing.

Aspire to role model the importance of wellbeing by looking after yourself; this in turn will allow you to support your students.

YOUR FINAL REFLECTIVE QUESTION

1. Do you spend enough time thinking about and taking action to support your own wellbeing? What do you do to ensure your bucket doesn't overflow?

FURTHER READING

Bethune, A and Kell E (2020) *A Little Guide for Teachers: Teacher Wellbeing and Self-care (A Little Guide for Teachers)*, Corwin

DfE (2019) Relationships education, relationships and sex education (RSE) and health education, https://assets.publishing.service.gov.uk/media/62cea352e90e071e789ea9bf/relationships_education_rse_and_health_education.pdf

Eyre, C (2016) *The Elephant in the Staffroom: How to Reduce Stress and Improve Teacher Wellbeing*, Routledge

PHE/NAHT (2014) The link between pupil health and wellbeing and attainment, https://assets.publishing.service.gov.uk/media/5a7ede2ded915d74e33f2eba/HT_briefing_layoutvFINALvii.pdf

BIBLIOGRAPHY

Akerlof GA and Kranton RE (2010) *Identity Economics: How Our Identities Shape Our Work, Wages, and Well-Being* (Princeton University Press)

Annual Report of the Chief Medical Officer (2013) https://assets.publishing.service.gov.uk/media/5a8034e0e5274a2e87db87a0/CMO_web_doc.pdf

Banerjee R, Weare K and Farr W (2013) Working with 'Social and Emotional Aspects of Learning' (SEL): Associations with school ethos, pupil social experiences, attendance, and attainment. BERA, https://doi.org/10.1002/berj.3114

Beltman S, Mansfield CF and Price A (2011) Thriving not just surviving: A review of research on teacher resilience. *Educational Research Review*, 6(3), 185-207

Blackmore S (2012) Ted Talk, https://www.youtube.com/watch?v=6zVS8HIPUng

Blackmore S (2019a) *Inventing Ourselves: The Secret Life of the Teenage Brain* (Black Swan)

Blackmore S (2019b) The neuroscience of the teenage brain, https://www.youtube.com/watch?v=yQXhFa8dRCI

Briner R and Dewberry C (2007) Report for worklife support on the relation between well-being and climate in schools and pupil performance, https://www.teachertoolkit.co.uk/wp-content/uploads/2014/07/5902birkbeckwbperfsummaryfinal.pdf

CASEL (2024) Collaborative for Academic, Social, and Emotional Learning, https://casel.org/

Chameleon PDE (2024) How do you compare? Report comparing How Are You? Student voice data in the academic years 2022/23 and 10123/24, https://www.chameleonpde.com/

Clark J (2024) *Teaching One Pagers, Evidence-informed summaries for busy educational professionals* (John Catt from Hodder Education)

Collie RJ, Shapka JD and Perry NE (2012) School climate and social-emotional learning: Predicting teacher stress, job satisfaction, and teaching efficacy. *Journal of Educational Psychology*, 104(4), 1189-1204

Day, C., & Gu, Q. (2009). *Teacher emotions: Well-being and resilience in teachers*. Open University Press.

DfE (2019) Relationships education, relationships and sex education (RSE) and health education, https://assets.publishing.service.gov.uk/media/62cea352e90e071e789ea9bf/Relationships_Education_RSE_and_Health_Education.pdf

Education Endowment Foundation (n.d.) Teaching and learning toolkit, https://educationendowmentfoundation.org.uk/education-evidence/teaching-learning-toolkit

Education Support (2023). *Teacher Wellbeing Index 2023*. Retrieved from https://www.educationsupport.org.uk/resources/for-organisations/research/teacher-wellbeing-index/?gad_source=1&gclid=CjOKCQiA-5a9BhCBARIsACwMkJ7yiW2_rEr5

Edurio (2024) Staff wellbeing in academies, https://home.edurio.com/insights/staff-welbeing-in-schools-2024

Forbes (2024) 12 Top countries for women's rights and gender equality, according to 2024 reports, https://www.forbes.com/sites/kathleenpeddicord/2024/11/12/top-12-countries-for-womens-rights-and-gender-equality/

Bibliography

Hammet, E (n.d.) Surprising statistics concerning sport related injuries in children, https://firstaidforlife.org.uk/sport-related-injuries-in-children/ (accessed 2024)

Harding S, Morris R, Gunnell D, Ford T, Hollingworth W, Tilling K and Brockman R (2019) Is teachers' mental health and well-being associated with students' mental health and well-being? *Journal of Affective Disorders*, 242, 180–187

Hoyle, A and McGeeney E (2020) *Great Relationships and Sex Education: 200+ Activities for Educators Working with Young People* (Routledge)

Jones SC, Andrews K and Frances K (2017) combining social norms and social marketing to address underage drinking: Development and process evaluation of a whole-of-community intervention, https://pmc.ncbi.nlm.nih.gov/articles/PMC5249059/

Marmot M, Goldblatt P, Allen J, et al. (2021) Fair society, healthy lives (The Marmot Review), 10 years on. https://www.instituteofhealthequity.org/resources-reports/marmot-review-10-years-on/the-marmot-review-10-years-on-full-report.pdf

National Foundation for Educational Research (2021). Teacher labour market in England 2019. https://bibliotheek.ehb.be:2235/fulltext/ED615303.pdf

Perkins HW (2002) Social norms and the prevention of alcohol misuse in collegiate contexts, https://www.jsad.com/doi/abs/10.15288/jsas.2002.s14.164

PHE/NAHT (2014) The link between pupil health and wellbeing and attainment, https://assets.publishing.service.gov.uk/media/5a7ede2ded915d74e33f2eba/HT_briefing_layoutvFINALvii.pdf

Popham C (2024) Behind the knife crime statistics: Understanding children who carry weapons, https://youthendowmentfund.org.uk/behind-the-knife-crime-statistics-understanding-children-who-carry-weapons/

Public Health England/National Association of Headteachers (2014) The link between pupil health and well-being and attainment: a briefing for head teachers, governance and staff in education settings, https://assets.publishing.service.gov.uk/media/5a7ede2ded915d74e33f2eba/HT_briefing_layoutvFINALvii.pdf

Public Health England (2024) The link between pupil health and wellbeing and attainment, https://assets.publishing.service.gov.uk/media/5a7ede2ded915d74e33f2eba/HT_briefing_layoutvFINALvii.pdf

Ross A (2024) Revealed: Schools facing 'national emergency' of knife crime with four attacks every week, https://www.independent.co.uk/news/uk/crime/knife-crime-attacks-schools-election-b2561071.html

Samaritans (2024) Suicide rates across the UK, https://www.samaritans.org/about-samaritans/research-policy/suicide-facts-and-figures/latest-suicide-data/

Sandel MJ (2013) *What Money Can't Buy: The Moral Limits of Markets* (Penguin)

Stastista, only fans data (2024) https://www.statista.com/statistics/1339649/onlyfans-posts/

Statutory guidance: Relationships and sex education (RSE) and health education (2019; revised 2021) Department for Education, https://www.gov.uk/government/publications/relationships-education-relationships-and-sex-education-rse-and-health-education

Tait J (2020) *Teaching Rebooted: Using the Science of Learning to Transform Classroom Practice* (Bloomsbury)

World Economic Forum (2023) Future of jobs 2023: These are the most in-demand skills now – and beyond, https://www.weforum.org/agenda/2023/05/future-of-jobs-2023-skills/

World Economic Forum (2024) Global Gender Gap 2024, https://www3.weforum.org/docs/WEF_GGGR_2024.pdf

World Health Organisation (2024) Health behaviour in school-aged children, https://www.who.int/europe/initiatives/health-behaviour-in-school-aged-children-(hbsc)-study

INDEX

Note: For figure citations, page numbers appear in *italics*. For table citations, page numbers appear in **bold**. 'App' is an abbreviation of Appendices.

A levels 36
abortion 117, 125
abuse: domestic 77, 79; emotional 76, 78, 80; honour-based 75, 77, 79; online 76, 78, 80; peer-on-peer 74, 76, 78-9; of power 42; sexual 74, 77, 79, 125
access to justice 116
active learning 105; methods 37-8; value of 35; skills 25
active teaching: methods 37-9, 111
adolescence 12, 48-64; adaptation 53; brain development 48-9; embarrassment 119-20; facts 53; hormones 50; patience 51-2, 121-2; peer influence 50-1; positivity 53; risky behaviour 51; space requirements 121-2; substance use 49, *52*, *82*; teenage perspectives 121; understanding and support for 49-50, 53-4; *see also* embarrassment; puberty 12
Affordable Schools Network 5
age 118
'agree/disagree with' statements 22-3
AI *see* artificial intelligence (AI)
Akerlof, G. A. 139
alcohol 6, 49, 75, 77, 79, 159; adolescent use *52*, *82*; consumption 32, 83-5; education 11
algorithms: understanding *102*
'all hands up' cold calling 106
Allison, S. 107
ambition 30
Annual Report of the Chief Medical Officer 153
anonymous participation 106
anxiety 33, 49, 96-7, *97*; health 97; social 97
artificial intelligence (AI) 27, 30, 35, 91

ask-it basket 38
assault: online exposure to 99; physical 77; physical 78; sexual 77, 79, 125, 133
assessment 17-19; knowledge-based 22; PSHE model *18*, 20
attitude continuum statements 38
attitudes: knowledge and skills *32*
attributes 29-30
awards 5-6

Banerjee, R. 157
Bath & North East Somerset 5
Beltman, S. 156
Bethune, A. 163
bi-sexuality 23
big data 35
Blackmore, S. 50, 54-5
bladder and bowel health 5-6
blood donation *16*
boredom 158
'bottom-up' approach 4, 8
Brabban, A. 158
brain development 48-9
breathing techniques 59
Breeze, E. 54
Briner, R. 155
Brookfield, Stephen D. 73
budgeting skills 138-9, 147, *148*, 149
bullying 76, 78-9, 130; actions against/anti-bullying 42, *148*; online 15, 76, 78-9; types of 6, 42; verbal 12

calming techniques *see* emotions
cannabis 21, 51; adolescent use *52*, *82*; legal position of 128; workshops 6

car maintenance 149
carbon footprint *see* environmental concerns
card sort 38
career aspirations: shifts in 140-1
carers: resources for 7
carousel 38
Carragher, C. 71-2
case studies 111
CASEL 33, 39, 66
catastrophising: avoidance of 110
CDP *see* continuous professional development (CPD)
challenge: low stakes, high challenge 107
Chameleon PDE *x*, 6, 10, 15, 17, 51, 68, 85-8
change: fast pace of 2
child criminal exploitation 75-6, 78
child sexual exploitation 76-7, 79
citizenship studies 74
Clark, J. 107, 112
coercion 76, 78-9, 95
cognitive skills *34*
Collie, R. J. 156
community development 7
community safety 116
computing 74
concentration span 103-4
concerns about health 98
confidence *30*
conflict resolution 31
connected learning 22, 25
connections 108; activities *see* 'find the connections' activity; power of 109
consent: active consent definition 134-5, 137; sexual *11*, *12*, 23, 75, 77, 78, 133
continuous professional development (CPD): concept of 32; confidence-building 125; importance of 124; knowledge and confidence 72; limitations 65; regular programme 67; staff resources 6; teacher embarrassment 123; teacher wellbeing 157-8, 160; whole-school approach 67
continuum activities 28
contraception 125, 157
controversy 2
cooking 149
counselling services 161
county lines 75-6, 78
COVID-19 pandemic: recovery 6; socialisation, lack of 88; suicide, effect on 91; teacher stress 161

creative activities 29
creativity 48, 149
current self *101*
customer service 35
CVs (Curriculum Vitae) 151-2

dating 60-4
Day, C. 155
debate 38
debt: guidance on 147
deep learning 19-20
Department of Education (DfE) 153, 163
depression 49
design and technology skills 142-3
desirable difficulty 108
Dewberry, C. 155
Diamond 9 template *31*, 38
digital safety *see* online safety
disability 13, 118
discrimination 76, 78, 80, 157; gender-based 118; legal 116
disrespectful behaviour 12
distanced scenarios 38
distraction techniques 59
diversity 43, 72
domestic violence 77, 79, 116
dot voting 28
'draw and write' 38
dreams: upsetting 97, 99, *99*
drugs 75, 77, 79
drugs: adolescence *52*, *82*; education 11, *148*; *see also* cannabis
Duke of Edinburgh award 36
Dwek, C. S. 56
eating: disorders 76, 78, 80; healthy *148*
Education Endowment Foundation 153
Education Support (charity) 154
Edurio 154
embarrassment 119-37, 57; activities to minimise 122; answering personal questions 127-8; answering questions immediately 128; distancing techniques 122; gossip 123; humour strategies 120; management strategies 121-2; parents 126; patience 121-2; personal views 123; physical symptoms of 119; quality resources 124; refusal to teach topic 124-5; resources 133; sharing personal information 122-3; space requirements 121-2; student 119; teacher 123-4; teacher errors 122-3; teenage perspectives 119-21; thinking time for

answering questions 128-9; tricky questions or comments 126-7; tricky topics 125
emotional and mental health 88-90; statistics 89-90
emotional intelligence 149; value of 35
emotional learning *see* social and emotional learning
emotional regulation 108
emotionally based school non-attendance 5
emotions 56; breathing techniques 59; calming strategies 58-9; confused feelings 23; dating and 60-1; distraction 59; exercise 59; extreme 49-50; frustration 62; high 57-8; journaling 59; management strategies 29, 98; managing 'strong' 57; meditation 59; mindfulness 59; physical responses to 58; respect and 61-2; strategies for managing 64; strength of adolescent 64; turmoil 59-60; words 59; *see also* mental health
empathy 29, *30*
empowering opportunities 140
English: as a first language 28; as an additional language 5, 72
environmental concerns 98, **98**
Equality Act (2010): protected characteristics 26, 42, 76, 78, 80, 125
equality: equal opportunities 114; equal responsibilities 114; equal rights 114; factors by country 115-16, *116*; gender 113-15; health inequality 9; inequality, tackling 113; more equal societies 116-17, *116, 117*
ethnic minorities 13
ethnicity 6
European Union (EU) 115
Everard, S. 74
Everyone's Invited 74
examination 98; workload **98**
excellent teaching principles 107
exercise 59; benefits of *11*, 31
expertise: lack of 1
exploitation 140
Eyre, C. 163

families: types of 31
Feast, J. 37-8
female genital mutilation (FGM) 75, 125, 130
femicide 85
films 28

financial exploitation 95
financial literacy 138, 144-6; finance skills 139; gamification 146; resources for improving 144-7
financial rewards: online 140
'find the connections' activity *30*, 40-2
'find the word' activity 43-4
first aid 143, 146-7, *148*, 149; context and consolidation 143-4; embeddedness within PSHE 143-4; timing 143-4
'fly on the wall' scenarios 111
Food for Life 6
food shopping 149
Forbes 115
fraud 142
friendships 23
fundraising events 29

gambling 6, 86-7, 142; statistics 86
gang culture 75-6, 78
gap year 36
Garden International School, Malaysia 71-2
gender 6, 23, 50, 93; emotional and mental health *89-90*; equality by country 113-15; equality, UN definition of 113-14; relevance by 85-6; *see also* LGBTQ+ education; women
gifts 30
Gillick competence 137
Gilmour, J. 56
graffiti wall 38
gratitude *30*, 59
grooming 76-7, 79
ground rules: importance of 104-5
group work 38, 40
Gu, Q. 155
Guardian newspaper 53-4

Hammet, E. 144
harassment 15; non-sexual 76-7, 79; *see also* bullying; sexual harassment
Harding, S. 155
Health and Safety Executive 155
health schools status 5-6
health 76; academic attainment and 5; anxiety 98; epidemics 14; long-term outcomes 3; population-based statistics 110; promotion 3, 8; *see also* sexual health
high expectations 108
Hohnen, B. 56
homelessness 75, 77-8

homophobia 12
homosexuality 23
hormones 48, 50; sex 50; stress 50; see also puberty
hot topic interviews 38
household chores 149
'How are You?' Pupil voice survey 6, *68*, 71, 133, 138, *148*
Hoyle, A. 39, 132
humility *30*, 109
Humpston, M. 144-6

images: inappropriate 6
impulses 49
inclusivity see diversity
Independent School's Inspectorate (ISI) 74
Independent newspaper 84
initiations/dares 75, 77, 79
interculturalism 71

Jigsaw Families 7
Jones, B. 92-4
Jones, S. C. 83
journaling 24, 59, 151

Kahoot 28
Kell, E. 163
Khan Academy 147
kindness *30*
knife crime 75-6, 78, 84-5, *85*, 110
knowledge 29-30; consolidation of 15-17; knowledge-based assessment 22; recall 15-17; retaining 10; skills and attitudes *32*
Kranton, R. E. 139

Labour Force Survey 155
language 12; homophobic 12; positive use of *18*; transphobic 12; vaping habits 81; see also English
leadership: poor 66
lectures: interpretations of 110; lecture-style lessons 103, 112
Lemov, D. 105, 112
Lewis, M. 147
LGBTQ+ education 13, 76, 78, 80, 118, 123, 125, *148*
life skills 17, 108, 138-52; beyond money, finance, and tax 142-3; budgeting 139; challenges 151; definition of 144; finance 139; global education perspective 144-6; money 139; most important 149-51; preparedness 141; progression 142; relevance 142; resources 148; self-identity, darker side of 139; tax 139; top five *148*, 148-9; see also first aid
lifelong learning 32

macroeconomic theory 103
management skills *34*
Marmot, M. 1, 9
marriage 137; forced 75, 77, 79
maternal mortality ratio 116
maternity allowance 115
maternity leave 115
mathematics 103, 108, 145
maturity 51, 88; variability of 12
McAleese, C. 5-8
McGeeney, E. 39, 132
McPhee, S. L. 132
meditations 59
menstrual periods 130
mental health 3, 93, *148*, 149; boys, support for 6; illness 49, 76, 78, 80; issues 48, 56; online safety and 95; resources 157; strategies 56, 76, 78, 80, 158; young champions programme trial 7; see also emotional and mental health; wellbeing
Mentimeter 28, 106
mind maps 38
mindfulness 59
mingle bingo 38
misogyny 12, 67, 73-5, 77, 79, 107, 112-13, 128, 139, 157
money: guidance on 147; skills 139
motivation *30*
murder 64, 99
Murphy, T. 56
music 28
Muslim population 84

National Foundation for Educational Research 155
natural disasters 14
neglect 77, 79
negotiation skills 25
networking 5
neurodivergence 119
New York Times quiz 40
newsletters 6
Newton, H. 64
NHS Trust 144
'no opt out' 105

Ofsted 6, 74
online influencers 139-40
online messaging: negative 99
online safety 11, 15, 157; blocking and reporting content 99; lessons 11; scams 95, 142
OnlyFans 140
open evenings 24
oral health 16
organ donation 16

pandemic see COVID-19 pandemic
Papyrus 95
parent's evening meetings 68
parents 126; resources for 7
parliamentary representation 116, *116*
paternity leave 115
patience 51-2
peer approval 50, 53, 56, 110
peer group behaviour: perception of 19
peer influence 4, 50-1, 75, 77, 79
peer judgment 98, **98**
peer relationships 48
peer support 156
perfectionism 162
Perkins, H. W. 83
Personal Development Education programme 17
personal hygiene *16*
personal safety 75, 77-8
Personal, Social, Health and Economic (PSHE): assessment model *18*; auditing provisions 74-80; deeper learning 19; effective measures 105; effective pedagogy 103-18; good quality, barriers to 65-6; important role of 8; Leads Network 5; monitoring progress 10-21; outcomes for 31; pedagogy for 104; programme plan 14-15; relevance, importance of 81-102 reputation of 2; resources 6; school leadership 67-70; topic five topics 11; tricky topics 125; usefulness of 70, 71; variety in lessons 28-9
PHE/NAHT 153, 163
physical activity levels 5; see also exercise
podcasts 29
Popham, C. 84
pornography 76-7, 79, 87-8, 125, 132, *148*, 149; statistics 87
positivity 53

posters 29
pranks 36
pregnancy: termination see abortion; unintended 133
prejudice 76, 78, 80
presentation skills 25
pressure situations 31
privacy: invasion of 161; protection of 127
problem-solving skills 149
professional learning communities (PLCs) 71
profile: lack of 65-6
projective techniques 38
property: buying and renting 141, 149
PSHE see Personal, Social, Health and Economic (PSHE)
puberty *11*; hormone fluctuations 50; physical changes 11-12, *16*, 50, 56
Public Health England 5, 9
Public Health teams 4
Pugh, V. M. 132
pupil voice survey see 'How are You?' Pupil voice survey
puppets 38

qualitative data 13-14
questionnaires 38, 72
quizzes 38, 40

race 118
radicalisation 75, 77-8
ranking attitudes 38
rape 77, 79
Rees, J. 153
reflections: healthy relationships 24-5; individual 24; personal 31, 39, 55, 73, 94, 112, 131, 146-7
relationships: abusive 64; healthy 11, 22-6, *148*; intimate 12, 133, 136; peer, focus on 48; romantic 22-3, 60-1, 122, 136; skills 33; unsafe 64
Relationships, Sex and Health Education (RSHE) 1, 6, 11; Guidance from the Secretary of State 153; high quality 157
religious education 66, 74
religious views 124, 129
reluctant students 109
repairs 149
repetition 20
resilience 6, 49

resource limitations 66
respect 109; for community 31; mutual 69; peer-to-peer 68, 69; respecting others 25, 61-2; staff-to-student 68
responsible decision-making 33-4
risk-taking 19, 49; risky behaviour 51
role models: importance of 65-80; staff as positive 68; teachers as 68, 68-9, 73, 108; top tips 108-9
role-play 38
Ross, A. 84
RSHE see Relationships, Sex and Health Education (RSHE)

safety: online see online safety; personal see personal safety
Samaritans 91, 95
Sandel, M. J. 142, 147
scare tactics 110
school culture: positive 154; supportive and inclusive 156
science studies 74
search engines 101-2
SEEAT 54
self-absorption 50
self-awareness 33, 29
self-belief 30
self-confidence 97, 157
self-defence 149
self-discipline 150-1
self-efficacy 34
self-esteem 30, 31
self-harm 6, 76, 78, 80
self-identity 23, 48, 119-21, 139
self-image 139
self-management 33
self-regulation 108
self-talk, positive 98
self-worth 29, 30
Senior Mental Health Leads Network 5
service orientation 35
sex: education 7, 120, 124-6, 133, 148; legal implications 137; negative reasons for having 134-5; positive reasons for having 134-5; reasons for having 133-5; sexual behaviour, appropriacy of 135-6; see also consent; pregnancy
sex offenders register 110
sexting 75, 77, 79
sextortion 95
sexual harassment 73-5, 77, 79, 125, 133

sexual health 76-7, 79, 125, 157
sexuality 23, 50, 93; see also gender; LGBTQ+ education
sexually explicit content 140; see also pornography
sexually inappropriate behaviour 36
sexually transmitted infections (STIs) 125, 130, 133
single-sex schools 129-31
skills 23-5, 29-30; cognitive 34; design and technology 142-3; development 29; emerging 35; future leaders 35; knowledge and attitudes 32; management 34; relationship 33; technology 34; top employers 34; see also life skills
slavery: modern day 75, 77-8
sleep: importance of 49-50, 56
smoking 14, 51, 110, 159; adolescent use 52, 82; workshops 6; see also tobacco; vaping
social and emotional learning (SEL) 32-4, 37-9, 66, 71
social awareness 33, 29
social media 31, 50, 57, 59, 62, 101; algorithms 101-2; echo chamber 101; over-exposure to 98; see also online safety
social mobility 3
social norms theory 4
socialisation 88, 99
'son bias' 116
special educational needs (SEN) 38
sports injuries 144
squeezed curriculum 1-2
Squirrel 146
staff confidence 65
Staff Wellbeing in Academies 154
staff wellbeing see teacher wellbeing
stalking 64, 76-7, 79
Statista 140
STEM career choices 16
stem cell donation 16
stem sentences 38
stress: buckets 158-61, 161; coping with 33; de-stressors 158-9; false de-stressors 159; management strategies 159; reactions to 48; reduction in teachers 161-2; relaxants 159, 159; scale 160; stressors and relaxation techniques 159; work-related 155
student consultation 67
student councils 14
student panels 14

student voice 6, 72; power of 3-5; see also pupil voice survey
substance use 52, 75, 82; see also alcohol; drugs
successful lessons 29
suicide 78, 80, 91; charities 91; lesson delivery 91; organisations 95
summer romances 60-1
surveys 38
Swindon Borough Council 6; case study 5-8
Swindon Community Health Service 6-7
Swindon Healthy Schools 5-6
Swindon Public Health Team 6
Swindon Schools Mental Health and Emotional Wellbeing 5
Swindon and Wiltshire Asthma Friendly Schools 5
systems thinking 35

Tait, J. 19, 20
talent management 35
Tate, A. 139
tax 148, 149; life skills 139
teacher wellbeing 153-63; benefits 154; contributions to 154-6; government policies 156; practical support 158; reduction of 154-6; statistics 154; statutory expectations 157; stress buckets 158-61; stress reduction 161-2; supportive and inclusive school culture 156; Teacher Wellbeing Index (2023) 154
teachers: as role models 108; goals for students 30-2; influence of 67-9; newly qualified 129-31; wellbeing of see teacher wellbeing
team challenges 38
technology skills 34
TED Talks 103
tenacity 30
Tharby, A. 107
'think, pair, share' 38
thinking: abstract 48; complex processes 48; critical 72
thought shower 38
time constraints 92-4
time management 150
tobacco 21, 49, 75, 77, 79, 159; 'big tobacco' manipulation video 21; damaging effects of 31; education 11, 14; see also smoking
topics: 'hot topic' interviews 38; life skills 148, 148-9; progression across age ranges 16; repetitive 10-12; top five 11; tricky 125

trafficking 75, 77-8; see also slavery: modern
training: identified pupil needs 6-7
transphobia 12
Turkington, D. 158
TV series 28

understanding teenagers see adolescence
unfair comparison 98
United Nations (UN): gender equality, definition of 113-14
upskirting 76-7, 79
'upstream' approach 88

vaccinations 16
value-based decisions 32
values 29-30
vaping 6, 21, 51, 75, 77, 79, 81-3, 110; adolescent use 52, 82; workshops 6; see also smoking
variety 27-47; PSHE lessons 28-9
vocational qualifications 36
vulnerability 109

WEF see World Economic Forum (WEF)
wellbeing: academic attainment and 5; emotional 76, 78, 80; mental 6; questionnaires 72; teachers/staff see teacher wellbeing
'What happens next?' Scenarios 111
WHO see World Health Organisation (WHO)
wholesale instruction 110
women: abortion rights 117; breaking down stereotypes 117; children and careers 117; erosion of rights 117; maternal mortality 116; maternity rights 115; political violence against 116; senior representation of 117; violence towards 73-4; women's services 7; see also gender
word activities see 'find the word' activity; word searches
word searches 44-7
work-life balance 161-2
working with others 34
World Economic Forum (WEF) 34, 117
world events 97-8; frightening nature of 98
World Health Organisation (WHO) 83, 95; alcohol consumption statistics 83

younger self 100
Youth Endowment Fund 84, 95, 99
YouTube 103, 142

For Product Safety Concerns and Information please contact our EU
representative GPSR@taylorandfrancis.com
Taylor & Francis Verlag GmbH, Kaufingerstraße 24, 80331 München, Germany

www.ingramcontent.com/pod-product-compliance
Lightning Source LLC
Chambersburg PA
CBHW082100230426
43670CB00017B/2906